我的家乡中国陕西省，就位于古丝绸之路的起点。站在这里，回顾历史，我仿佛听到了山间回荡的声声驼铃，看到了大漠飘飞的袅袅孤烟。这一切，让我感到十分的亲切。

——习近平

My home town is in Shaanxi, which is the starting point of the ancient Silk Road. Standing on this land and reviewing history, I seem to hear camel bells echoing in valleys, and see smoke curling upward above the great desert. All these are fairly familiar to me.

—Xi Jinping

Zhonghua Genmai Wenhua Shaanxi

中华根脉
文化陕西

2022
中国陕西

2022 CHINA SHAANXI

陕西省人民政府新闻办公室 编
Information Office of Shaanxi Provincial People's Government

陕西新华出版传媒集团
陕 西 人 民 出 版 社

引言
Introduction

了解中国从陕西开始

To Learn about China, One must Begin from Shaanxi

陕西是一个美丽的地方，也是一个神奇的地方。

这里生态优美，宜居宜游。陕西北部是沟峁纵横的黄土高原，中部是沃野千里的关中平原，南部是峰峦叠翠的秦巴山区。全省纵跨长江、黄河两大流域，绵延 1600 多千米的秦岭是我国南北方的分界线，陕西的母亲河渭河是黄河的最大支流，发源于陕西的汉江是长江的最大支流。陕西风光秀丽，有很多美景：壶口瀑布波涛翻滚，西岳华山云蒸霞蔚，太白高峰六月积雪，洽川湿地芦荡万顷，秦巴深处鸟语花香。南北方的美景在这里相遇，

Shaanxi is a beautiful place, and also a miraculous place.

Shaanxi, boasting ecological charm to live and travel, combines the ravine-dotted Loess Plateau in the north, the flat and fertile Guanzhong Plain in the center, the mountainous Qinling-Daba Mountain Range in the south, and spans the basins of the Yangtze River and the Yellow River. The 1,600-plus km long Qinling Mountain Range is the great divide between the northern and southern parts of China. The Weihe River, the mother river of Shaanxi, is the largest tributary of the Yellow River. The Hanjiang River, rising in Shaanxi province, is the largest tributary of the Yangtze River. Shaanxi, boasting its gorgeous sceneries, is renowned for various beautiful landscapes such as the surging and roaring Hukou Waterfall, steep Huashan Mountain perennially capped with clouds, the snowy peaks of Mount Taibai in June, the lush reeds of Qiachuan Wetland, and the chirping birds and fragrant flowers in Qinling-Daba Mountain Range. Here the northern

呈现出瑰丽多姿、如诗如画的怡人景象。

这里历史悠久，文化灿烂。这里是中华民族和华夏文明的重要发祥地之一，有蓝田猿人、半坡遗址、轩辕黄帝陵等远古历史遗迹，有周、秦、汉、唐等 10 多个政权或朝代上千年的建都史，共有不可移动文物49058处、馆藏文物774万多件。在这里写就的众多汉赋、唐诗中，蕴含着中华民族的价值理念、道德规范和治国智慧。“看五千年中国到陕西”，是人们对陕西悠久历史和厚重文化的形象描述。

这里也是一片红色的土地。陕北是党中央和中央红军长征的落脚点，也是八路军奔赴抗日前线的出发点。延安是党中央战斗生活了 13 个春秋的地方。老一辈革命家和老一代共产党人在这里培育形成的延安精神，是我们党的宝贵精神财富。“几回回梦里回延安，双手搂定宝塔山。”越来越多的人来到这里，接受党的优良传统和作风教育，汲取不忘初心、牢记使命的精神力量。

这里科教资源富集，创新实力

scenery is integrated with the southern scenery to showcase a majestic and picturesque view.

Boasting a long history and brilliant culture, Shaanxi is one of the important cradles of the Chinese nation and culture. There are some ancient sites such as the Lantian Ape-men Site, Banpo Site, Mausoleum of the Yellow Emperor, etc. Over 10 powers and dynasties established their capitals in Shaanxi, including Zhou, Qin, Han and Tang. There are 49,058 immovable cultural relics and over 7.74 million collections of cultural relics. Many of the Han-fus and Tang poems written here contain the values, ethics, norms and wisdom of the Chinese nation. "From Shaanxi, one can know about Chinese history for 5,000 years." This is a vivid description of Shaanxi's profound history and culture.

This is a red revolutionary land. Northern Shaanxi is the foothold of the CPC Central Committee and the Central Red Army's Long March, as well as the starting point of the Eighth Route Army's rush to the frontline of resistance against Japanese aggression. Yan'an is the place where the CPC Central Committee has fought and lived for 13 years. Yan'an spirit, cultivated by the older generation revolutionary leaders and Communists, is our Party's precious spiritual wealth. "Several times back to Yan'an in my dreams, I put my arms around Mount Baota." More and more people are coming here to receive education of the Party's fine traditions and working style for strengthening the spiritual power to remain true to our original aspiration and keep our mission firmly in hand.

Shaanxi boasts its enrichment in science and education resources and strong strength in innovation. In the 1950s and 1960s, a number of universities such as Jiaotong University, enterprises and research institutes moved westward, consolidating the position of Shaanxi as a major province of science and education. Today,

雄厚。20世纪五六十年代，交通大学等一批高校、企业、科研院所的西迁，奠定了陕西科教大省的地位。今天的陕西，有各类科研机构1500多家，高等院校100多所，航空航天、3D打印、5G移动通信等技术保持世界先进水平，“神舟”飞天、“嫦娥”探月、“蛟龙”潜海，都有陕西科技的坚强支撑。

这里区位优越，开放包容。陕西处于中国版图中心位置，自古以来就是我国重要的对外开放门户。西汉时期的公元前138年，陕西人张骞“凿空之旅”开启的丝绸之路构筑起东西方交往的重要通道，唐代长安城成为世界上第一个人口过百万的大都市。

来到陕西，可触摸中华民族生生不息的根脉，可尽览中华人文多姿多彩的风情，可感知中国变革行稳致远的律动。了解中国，从陕西开始！

Shaanxi is home to more than 1500 enterprises and research institutes, and more than 100 universities. Aerospace, 3D printing, 5G mobile communication and other technologies in Shaanxi maintain world-class level. Launch of Shenzhou spaceship into space, landing of Chang'e Lunar Satellite on the moon and deep-sea manned submersible Jiaolong are supported strongly by Shaanxi science and technology strength.

Shaanxi enjoys an excellent geographical location and an open and inclusive spirit. Located in the center of China's territory, Shaanxi has been an important gateway to the outside world since ancient times. In 138 B.C. of the Western Han Dynasty, Zhang Qian, born in Shaanxi, opened up the world-famous Silk Road, which has become an important route linking Asia with Europe. Chang'an city in the Tang Dynasty was the first metropolis in the world with a population of more than one million.

In Shaanxi, you can touch the roots and feel the pulse of a vigorous Chinese nation, see the colorful charm of Chinese culture, and experience the steady and profound rhythm of reform in China. Shaanxi is a good starting point to learn about China!

陕南田园生态

目 录

Contents

第二篇
青山绿水，持续发展
林间新绿一重重

Chapter Two
Lush Mountains and Lucid Waters for Sustainable Development
New Green Leaves Throbbing Among Branches

第三篇
蓬勃生机，开拓进取
晴空一鹤排云上

Chapter Three
Booming with Vitality and Forging Ahead
A Crane Flapping its Wings to the Clear Sky

第四篇

安居乐业，脱贫致富

丰年留客足鸡豚

Chapter Four

Living and Working in Peace, Shaking Off Poverty and Getting Rich

Ample Food for Guests in Good Years

第五篇
海纳百川，兼容并包
百川衮衮东赴海

Chapter Five
Embracing and All-inclusive
All Rivers Flowing East to the Sea

附录
Annex

陕西地理位置优越，地貌丰富多样，资源丰沛，是中华民族及华夏文明的重要发祥地之一，有周、秦、汉、唐等 10 多个政权或朝代在此建都，留下了无数历史文化遗产。黄帝陵、秦兵马俑、延安宝塔、秦岭、华山等是中华文明、中国革命、中华地理的精神标识和自然标识，“看五千年中国到陕西”，是人们对陕西悠久历史和厚重文化的形象描述。

Boasting advantageous location, varied landforms, and rich resources, Shaanxi is an important cradle of the Chinese nation and culture. Over 10 powers and dynasties established their capitals in Shaanxi, including the Zhou, the Qin, the Han, and the Tang Dynasties, leaving behind their countless historical and cultural relics. The Mausoleum of the Yellow Emperor, the Terracotta Warriors and Horses, Yan'an Pagoda, the Qinling Mountains, and Mount Hua are the spiritual and natural symbols of the Chinese civilization, the Chinese revolution, and the Chinese geography. "From Shaanxi, one can know about the Chinese history for 5,000 years." This is a vivid description of Shaanxi's profound culture.

›

Chapter One

第一篇

人杰地灵，底蕴深厚

长安回望绣成堆

Inspiring Place with Outstanding People and Profound Heritage

Viewed from Chang'an, Mount Li Seemed
a Piece of Embroidery

自然环境
Natural Environment

汉江支流

1. 地理位置 Geographical Location

陕西位于东经105° 29′ —111° 15′ 、北纬31° 42′ —39° 35′ 之间，地处中国内陆腹地，东邻山西、河南，西连宁夏、

Shaanxi is situated at the hinterland of China at longitude of 105° 29′ −111° 15′ east and latitude of 31° 42′ −39° 35′ north. It neighbors the provinces of Shanxi and Henan to the east, Ningxia Hui Autonomous Region and Gansu Province to the west, Sichuan Province,

甘肃，南抵四川、重庆、湖北，北接内蒙古，是连接中国东、中部地区和西北、西南的交通枢纽。中国的大地原点就在陕西省泾阳县永乐镇。

Chongqing Municipality and Hubei Province to the south, and Inner Mongolia Autonomous Region to the north. With convenient transportation links and a strategic location, it serves as a hub which connects eastern and central China with northwestern and southwestern China. The geodetic origin of China is found in Yongle Town, Jingyang County,

陕西在中国的地理位置示意图

陕西下辖西安、宝鸡、咸阳、铜川、渭南、延安、榆林、汉中、安康、商洛10个地级市和杨凌农业高新技术产业示范区；2020年陕西省常住人口为3952.9万人。

Shaanxi Province.

Shaanxi has jurisdiction over 10 prefecture-level cities, namely Xi'an, Baoji, Xianyang, Tongchuan, Weinan, Yan'an, Yulin, Hanzhong, Ankang and Shangluo, as well as the Yangling Agricultural Hi-tech Industries Demonstration Zone. It had a permanent registered population of 39.5 million in 2020.

陕西省行政区划简图

西岳华山

2. 地形地貌 Landform

陕西总面积 20.56 万平方千米，纵跨长江、黄河两大流域和中温、暖温、亚热三个气候带，自然形成了陕北、关中、陕南三大区域。地域南北狭长，地势南北高、中间

With a total area of 205,600 square kilometers, Shaanxi spans the basins of the Yangtze River and the Yellow River, covering intermediate, warm temperate and subtropical climatic zones. The province consists of three parts: Northern Shaanxi, Guanzhong, and Southern Shaanxi. Topographically, Shaanxi is long and narrow, with higher altitudes in both south and north and lower elevation in the middle. Within

退耕还林后的陕北

低，有高原、山地、平原和盆地等多种地形。因此陕西省各地气候、水文、地貌差异较大，特色鲜明。秦岭绵延 1600 多千米，是中国南北方的分界线。

the territory of Shaanxi, there are various landforms, such as plateaus, mountainous regions, plains and basins. Thus, the climate, hydrology and geomorphology vary across the province with distinctive characteristics. The over 1,600 km-long Qinling Mountains, are the great divide between the northern and southern parts of China.

延安市南泥湾

3. 丰沛资源 Rich Resources

陕西是中国的资源大省，已发现矿产138种。陕西矿产资源在全国占据重要位置，在占国民经济重要价值的15种重要矿产中，石油保有储量排全国第三位，煤、天然气、水泥灰岩保有储量均排全国第四位。陕西也因此成为国家西气东输、西电

As a key resource province of China, Shaanxi has 138 types of minerals and enjoys an important position in the country in terms of mineral resources. Among 15 important minerals of great significance in national economy, the retained reserve of petroleum ranks third in the country, while those of coal, natural gas and cement limestone all rank fourth. Therefore, Shaanxi has

延安煤油气资源综合利用项目

东送、西煤东运的重要能源基地。秦岭有野生种子植物3800余种，约占全国的15%。大熊猫、金丝猴、朱鹮、羚牛等119种濒危野生动物在此生息繁衍。陕南秦巴山区拥有丰富的水资源，开发水力发电潜力巨大，也是中国南水北调中线工程的水源涵养地。

become an important energy base for the west-to-east transmission of gas, electricity and coal in China. The Qinling Mountain Range is home to over 3,800 wild seed plants, accounting for about 15% of the national total, and 119 endangered animals, including the panda, the golden monkey, the crested ibis and the takin. The Qinling-Daba Mountainous Region in Southern Shaanxi is rich in water resources and has enormous potential for exploitation of hydropower. It is also a water source for the South-to-North Water Diversion Project.

历史文化 History and Culture

1. 悠久历史 Long History

中华人文始祖黄帝 5000 年前在陕西开创了中华文明，位于黄陵县的黄帝陵和位于宝鸡市的炎帝陵，是中华文明发祥地的重要标志。

中国历史上有西周、秦、汉、唐等 14 个王朝在陕西建都。秦朝是中国第一个中央集权的封建王朝。到西

Around 5,000 years ago, China's cultural ancestor, the Yellow Emperor, created the Chinese civilization in Shaanxi. The Yellow Emperor Mausoleum in Huangling County and Emperor Yandi's Mausoleum in Baoji City are prominent symbols of the birthplace of Chinese civilization.

Altogether 14 dynasties, including the Western Zhou, the Qin, the Han and the Tang, established their capitals in Shaanxi. The Qin Dynasty is the first unified feudal dynasty with a centralized political system in the history of

黄帝陵

汉时期，社会、经济、文化全面发展，汉唐丝绸之路从陕西开端。唐朝是中国历史上最强盛的王朝，都城长安不仅是当时中国政治、经济、文化的中心，更是国际闻名的大都市。

唐代以后，统治中心东移，陕西不再是中国的政治、经济中心，但在中国政治、经济和军事上仍占有重要地位，直到近代，一直是西部重镇。

China. The Western Han Dynasty witnessed the integrated development of the society, the economy and the culture. The Silk Road started from Shaanxi during the Han and the Tang dynasties. The Tang Empire was the most powerful among China's dynasties in history. Chang'an, the capital of Tang, was not only the political, economic and cultural center of China, but also a famous international metropolis.

After the Tang Dynasty, the center of governmental administration moved eastward. Shaanxi was no longer the political and economic center of China. However, Shaanxi still occupied an important position in politics, economy and military of China. Up to modern times, Shaanxi has been considered as a crucial area within the western part of China.

黄帝陵

2. 红色文化 Revolutionary Culture

陕西是红色革命沃土，延安是中国革命圣地。从 1935 年到 1948 年，延安是中共中央的所在地，是中国人民解放斗争的总后方。毛泽东等老一辈革命家亲

Shaanxi is the cradle of revolution, and Yan'an is the sacred land of Chinese revolution. From 1935 to 1948, Yan'an was the home of the CPC Central Committee and the overall rear base for the Chinese people's struggle for

宝塔山

手培育形成的延安精神，是中华民族精神宝库中的宝贵财富。延安现存革命旧址445处，其中宝塔山、凤凰山、杨家岭、枣园、王家坪、陕甘宁边区政府旧址等最为著名。

liberation. The Yan'an Spirit, nurtured by Mao Zedong and other revolutionary leaders of his generation, is a precious national treasure. Yan'an is home to 445 old revolutionary sites, among which the most famous ones are Mount Baota, Mount Fenghuang, Yangjialing, Zaoyuan, Wangjiaping and the site of Shaanxi-Gansu-Ningxia Border Government.

鲁迅艺术文学院

中央大礼堂

渭华起义旧址

薛家寨全景

陕甘边照金革命根据地位于铜川市耀州区。20 世纪 30 年代初，刘志丹、谢子长、习仲勋等老一辈革命家在这里开展革命活动，创建了以照金为中心的陕甘边革命根据地。陕甘边照金革命根据地的建立，点燃了西北革命的火种，为后来陕北革命根据地的建立创造了条件，在中国革命史上留下了光辉的一页。

2004 年，陕甘边革命根据地照金纪念馆正式开馆，被列为全国红色旅游经典景区。

The Zhaojin Revolutionary Base in Shaanxi-Gansu Border Region is located at Yaozhou District, Tongchuan City. In the early 1930s, the older generation revolutionary leaders, such as Liu Zhidan, Xie Zichang and Xi Zhongxun, bravely carried out revolutionary activities under extremely arduous conditions. They founded Shaanxi-Gansu Border Region Revolutionary Base with Zhaojin as the center. The establishment of Shaanxi-Gansu Border Region Revolutionary Base kindled the revolution in northwestern China, created conditions for the later Northen Shaanxi Revolutionary Base, and wrote a brilliant page in China's revolutionary history.

In 2004, the Memorial Hall of Zhaojin Revolutionary Base in Shaanxi-Gansu Border Region was officially opened. It is China's revolutionary scenic spot.

3. 民间文化 Folk Culture

陕西民间艺术丰富多彩，地域特色鲜明。许多项目被列入国家级非物质文化遗产名录。户县（西安市鄠邑区）、安塞（延安市安塞区）等县区被文化和旅游部命名为“全国民间绘画之乡”。2021年，榆林市榆阳区（陕北民歌）、延安市安塞区（安塞腰鼓）、渭南市华州区（皮影戏）、榆林市绥德县四十里铺镇（石雕）、铜川市印台区陈炉镇（陶艺）、渭南市富平县宫里

There are a variety of colorful folk art with outstanding regional features in Shaanxi. Many of them have been included in the list of National Intangible Cultural Heritage. The counties of Huxian(Huyi District, Xi'an) , Ansai (Ansai District,Yan'an), and other counties are named as "Hometown for National Folk Painting". In 2021, Yuyang District of Yulin City (famous for Northern Shaanxi folk songs), Ansai Ditrict of Yan'an City (famous for Ansai waist drums), Huazhou District of Weinan City (famous for shadow puppets), Sishilipu Township of Suide County, Yulin City(famous for stone carving), Chenlu Township of Yintai District in Tongchuan City (famous for ceramics), Gongli Township of Fuping County(famous for stone inscription), and Longjiang Street, Hantai District of Hanzhong City (famous for dragon dance) were included

秦腔现代戏《秦腔》

陕北腰鼓

镇（石刻）、汉中市汉台区龙江街道（龙舞）入选2021—2023年度“中国民间文化艺术之乡”。目前陕西省入选联合国教科文组织人类非物质文化遗产代表作名录的有西安鼓乐、中国剪纸、中国皮影戏三项。

秦腔是中国最具代表性的古老剧种之一，源于陕西、甘肃一带的民间曲调和宋金元的铙鼓杂剧，陕甘一带古为秦地，故称其为“秦腔”。又因其以枣木梆子为击节乐器，所以又叫“梆子腔”，俗称“乱弹”。

in the list of China's Home for Folk Culture and Art. Xi'an Drum Music, Paper-cutting and Shadow Puppets of China have been inscribed in the UNESCO Intangible Cultural Heritage List.

Qin Opera is one of the most representative old operas of China. It originated in the folk tunes and the timbrel opera of the Song, Jin and Yuan dynasties along Shaanxi and Gansu. The area around Shaanxi and Gansu was within the territory of the Kingdom of Qin, hence the name Qin Opera. As jujube wood bangzi (slit drum) is used for percussion in the performance, it is also called Bangzi Opera or Luantan (strum) by the locals.

Northern Shaanxi Ballads and Northern Shaanxi Paper-cutting enjoy rich Loess and frontier cultural features. Yangge Performance, Ansai Waist Drum and other traditional folk cultures spread from Northern Shaanxi to the rest of the

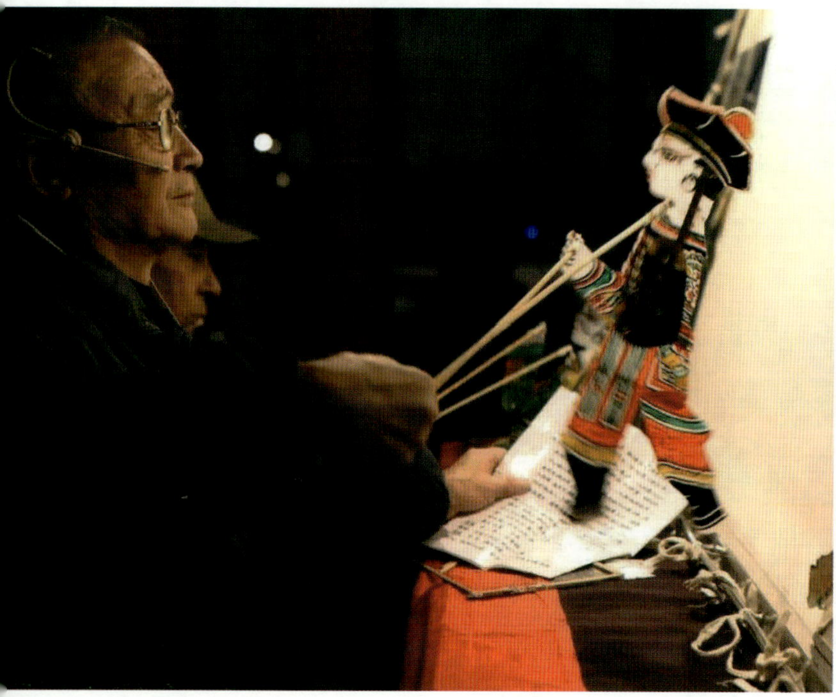

皮影戏

秦派内画鼻烟壶

秦腔绝技——吐火

陕北民歌、陕北剪纸具有浓郁的黄土文化和边塞文化特色；秧歌、安塞腰鼓等传统民间艺术也从陕北走向了世界。

华阴老腔曲风高亢豪迈、自在随性，是关中地区的代表性民间文化；社火是关中地区传统的民俗文娱活动；凤翔彩绘泥塑、凤翔木版年画和户县农民画等关中民间艺术体现了丰富多彩的民风民俗。

陕南地区的汉剧为京剧的形成做出过特殊贡献；紫阳民歌是陕南地区传统民歌中最具代表性的曲种。

world.

Huayin Laoqiang Opera enjoys vigorous, majestic, free and unconstrained features, representative of the folk culture in the Guanzhong Plain. Building Sacred Fire is a traditional folk custom and cultural activity in the area. Fengxiang Color-painted Clay Figurines, Fengxiang Xylograph New Year Pictures, Huxian County Farmers' Painting, and other folk arts in the Guanzhong Plain elaborately and vividly delineate the colorful customs with a plain style.

In Southern Shaanxi, Hanju Opera made special contributions to the formation of the Peking Opera. Ziyang Folk Song is the most representative among traditional folk songs.

4. 现代文化 Modern Culture

随着时代的发展，新兴的文化形态与陕西古老文化不断交融，创业咖啡街区为陕西创新创业注入了强大动力，成为展示城市新风貌的时尚地标。

陕西大剧院是西北地区首个国际

With the development of times, new cultural forms continuously integrate with ancient Shaanxi cultures. Xi'an Inno Start-up Wonderland infuses new vitality to the city's innovation and development, and has become a beautiful modern landmark for fashion.

Shaanxi Opera House, the first international,

西安蓝海风书店

化、专业化、综合性的大剧院，是展示古都文化魅力的重要窗口。

西安音乐厅是西北地区首屈一指的演出场馆，是享誉古城西安的文化地标。

professional and comprehensive theater in northwestern China, is an important window of Shaanxi to exhibit the cultural charm of its ancient capital.

Xi'an Concert Hall, the No.1 performance venue in northwestern China, is a renowned cultural landmark of the ancient city.

陕西大剧院

旅游胜地 Tourism Attractions

1. 人文之旅 Cultural Tourism

陕西人文旅游资源丰富，有黄帝陵、炎帝陵、秦始皇陵，以及汉唐帝陵等 70 多座帝王陵寝，以及众多国宝级古建筑。

中国现存规模最大、保存最完整的古代城垣——西安明城墙与护

Rich in cultural tourist resources, Shaanxi is home to over 70 mausoleums, including those of the Yellow Emperor, the Yandi Emperor, the Emperor Qinshihuang, and emperors of the Han and the Tang dynasties, as well as many ancient architectural complexes that can be regarded as national treasures.

城河及环城公园组成了西安市最具特色的一大景观。

位于市中心的钟楼与鼓楼是西安的标志性建筑，这两座明代建筑遥相呼应，蔚为壮观。

大雁塔与小雁塔是佛塔这种古印度佛寺的建筑形式融入华夏文化的典型物证。

华清宫也称华清池，位于西安市

Xi'an City Wall is the biggest and best-preserved ancient city wall still extant in China. The City Wall, together with the moat and annular park, forms a part of the fantastic scenery of Xi'an.

Situated at the center of Xi'an, the Bell Tower and the Drum Tower are landmark buildings of the city. The two majestic Ming Dynasty buildings echo each other from afar.

Both the Giant Wild Goose Pagoda and the Small Wild Goose Pagoda are representative physical evidence of the fusion of the ancient Indian Buddhist temples' architectural form with Chinese culture.

石峁遗址

榆林河滨公园

临潼区，其以唐明皇与杨贵妃缠绵的爱情故事和震惊中外的西安事变而蜚声中外。

大唐芙蓉园仿照唐代皇家园林建造，是中国第一个全方位展示盛唐风

Situated at Lintong District, Xi'an, the Huaqing Palace is also known as the Huaqing Pond. The palace is famed for the sentimental love story between Emperor Minghuang and his concubine Yang as well as the world-shaking Xi'an Incident.

The Tang Paradise was rebuilt according to the style of imperial gardens on its site of the Tang Dynasty. It

西安浐灞生态区

大明宫丹凤门遗址夜景

貌的大型皇家园林式文化主题公园。

从魏晋南北朝直到隋唐时期，长安一直是汉传佛教的活动中心，留下了法门寺、草堂寺等大量的祖庭寺庙。

is China's first large scale imperial garden-themed park that showcases the prosperity of the Tang Dynasty comprehensively.

Chang'an had been an important center of Buddhism from the Wei, Jin, Southern and Northern dynasties to the Sui and the Tang dynasties, and left many ancestral chambers and temples such as Famen Temple and Caotang Temple.

2. 山水之旅 Landscape Tourism

陕西地形狭长，地貌多样，特殊的地理环境，造就了陕西集高原沟峁、平原沃野和江南水乡风光于一体的多彩景象。

陕北山峦起伏，沟壑纵横，气象壮美；八百里秦川横亘关中，平川与黄土塬地交错铺排，相映成趣；陕南

Shaanxi Province, which is long and narrow in its topography, boasts a wealth of unique landforms, and integrates the northwestern scenery with the southern scenery to create a colorful and fantastic view.

Northern Shaanxi, boasting continuous mountains and valleys, is a majestic view. A 400 km-long section of the Qinling Mountain Range runs across the Guanzhong region where the plains and plateaus interlace with each other. Southern Shaanxi features green hills mirrored in

秦岭分水岭

青山绿水，风景如画，湖光山色相映生辉，峡谷溶洞遍布其间。

黄河、渭水、汉江风貌各异，既有雄浑壮阔的磅礴之美，也有蜿蜒曲折的秀丽旖旎。

秦岭位于中国中部，面积广大，气势磅礴，被誉为“国家中央公园”。

crystal rivers and picturesque sceneries dotted with lakes, mountains, canyons and water-eroded caves.

The Yellow River, the Weihe River and the Hanjiang River are characterized with their distinctive majestic beauty and winding charm.

The Qinling Mountain Range is located in central China as a vast, grand and majestic mountain, enjoying the fame of "National Central Park". In 2009, Shaanxi Qinling Zhongnanshan Geopark was listed as one of

2009 年，陕西秦岭终南山地质公园入选世界地质公园。太白山为秦岭山脉最高峰，自古以来就以高、寒、险、奇、富饶、神秘闻名于世。“太白积雪六月天”是著名的“长安八景”

the world geoparks. Mount Taibai, the highest peak of the Qinling Mountain Range, has been famed for its height, cold, steepness, fertility and mystery from ancient times. The so-called "Snow-capped Mount Taibai in Summer" is one of the top eight scenic attractions of Chang'an.

As one of the five famous mountains in China, the

汉中市龙头山景区雪景

之一。

华山是中国五大名山之一，海拔 2154 米。华山挺拔险峻，终年云蒸霞蔚，南接秦岭，北瞰黄渭，扼大西北进出中原的门户，素有“奇险天下第一山”之称。

Huashan Mountain has an altitude of 2,154 meters. Being an upright, steep mountain perennially capped with clouds, it connects the Qinling Mountains in the south, overlooks the Yellow River and the Weihe River in the north, and guards the plain in the Great Northwest. It has long been given the name of "The Number One Most Dangerous Mountain under Heaven".

3. 博物馆之旅
Museum Tourism

陕西被誉为中国天然历史博物馆，文化遗存丰富，文物点密度大、数量多、等级高，拥有中国各个历史时期具有代表性的文物古迹。陕西目前有 9 家国家一级博物馆，全面展示了三秦大地悠久的历史和灿烂辉煌的文化。

Shaanxi is known as China's "natural history museum". The cultural relics and historical ruins found here are concentrated, numerous and representative, encompassing almost every historical period in Chinese history. It is home to 9 state first-level museums which comprehensively reflect China's long history and splendid culture.

Shaanxi History Museum is China's first large scale national museum equipped with modern facilities. It

宝鸡中华石鼓园

陕西历史博物馆是中国第一座大型现代化国家级博物馆，馆藏文物时间跨度长达 100 多万年。其中汉唐金银器独步全国，唐墓壁画举世无双，被誉为“古都明珠，华夏宝库”。

秦始皇帝陵博物院是建立在秦

collects cultural relics with a time span of over one million years. The gold and silver wares of the Han and the Tang dynasties are the most exquisite in China. The murals in the Tang tombs are unrivaled in the world. The museum is honored "Pearl of Xi'an and treasure of China".

Emperor Qinshihuang's Terracotta Warriors and Horses Museum is built on the original pit for the terracotta warriors and horses. Thousands of vivid

陕西历史博物馆

兵马俑坑原址上的遗址性博物馆。博物馆的一、二、三号坑中发掘出了数千尊列为军阵的兵马俑。秦兵马俑是世界考古史上最伟大的发现之一，1987 年，联合国教科文组织将秦始皇陵及兵马俑坑列入世界遗产名录。

西安碑林博物馆是陕西创建最早的博物馆，以收藏、陈列和研究

terracotta warriors and horses with various postures in arrays were unearthed from the Pits No.1, 2 and 3. It is one of the greatest discoveries in the world archaeological history. In 1987, the UNESCO inscribed the Terracotta Warriors and Horses and the Mausoleum of Emperor Qinshihuang into the World Heritage List.

Xi'an Beilin Museum (Forest of Stone Steles Museum) is the earliest museum in Shaanxi. It mainly focuses on the collection, exhibition and research of steles, epitaphs and stone inscriptions. It gets the name Beilin from the Chinese meaning of forest of stone steles. The famous "Kaicheng Stone Sutra", "Stele for

延安革命纪念馆

历代碑刻、墓志及石刻为主，因碑石如林，故名碑林。著名的“开成石经”“大秦景教流传中国碑”“昭陵六骏”中的四骏等文物均藏于此馆。

延安革命纪念馆位于延安市宝塔区，是中华人民共和国成立后最早建立的革命纪念馆之一。它展出大量珍贵的革命文物、文献和照片，生动、形象地再现了老一辈革命家的光辉业绩。

the Spread of Cippus Nestorianism in China" and four steeds of the Six Steeds of Zhao Mausoleum are collected in the museum.

Yan'an Revolutionary Memorial, located in Baota District, Yan'an City, is one of the earliest revolutionary memorials built after the founding of the People's Republic of China. It exhibits numerous valuable revolutionary relics, literature and photos, vividly representing the older generation revolutionary leaders' glorious feats.

秦兵马俑
——世界八大奇迹之一
The Terracotta Warriors and Horses: One of the Eight Wonders of the World

秦俑，世界文化遗产，世界八大奇迹之一，全国重点文物保护单位。

贾谊在《过秦论》中以气势充沛的文笔记载了秦国历经几代君王，从崛起壮大到最后称霸的过程。而兵马俑就是横扫六国、称霸九州的大一统秦帝国强盛面貌的一个象征。

秦国的崛起称霸，离不开每一位秦兵秦将的英勇无畏，以及他们手中先进锋利的兵器，也离不开这种严密坚固的军阵布局。秦人结束了战国之后诸侯争霸、连年混战的局面，建立了中国历史上第一个大一统的帝国，对之后中国几千年的政治、经济、文化等都产生了深远的影响。

秦兵马俑不仅是一座丰富的军事宝库、一部立体的秦代兵书，同时也是一座辉煌的艺术殿堂。

Terracotta Warriors and Horses, world cultural heritage, known as one of the eight wonders of the world, is an important heritage site under state protection.

Jia Yi recorded the process of Qin state from rise to final hegemony through several generations of monarchs in his essay The Faults of Qin with vigorous writing style. Terracotta Warriors are a symbol of the powerful face of the Qin Empire, which eradicated six states and dominated China.

The rise of the state of Qin cannot be separated from the courage of every Qin soldier and general, as well as the advanced sharp weapons in their hands, nor can it be separated from such a tight and solid military array. The Qin people terminated the tangled warfare of vassals contending for hegemony after the Warring States Period and established the first unified empire in Chinese history, exerting a profound impact on China's subsequent politics, economy and culture for thousands of years.

Terracotta Warriors and Horses are not only a rich military treasure-

秦俑的军阵布局真实地模拟了秦代军队的屯聚阵列，这也使得这些艺术作品显得有血有肉。一个个陶俑形体高大，造型比例协调，神态栩栩如生，表情千人千面，无有雷同。这些陶俑甚至发丝分明，手指造型生动逼真，一个个或站或跪，或牵马或按剑，皆器宇轩昂，剽悍勇武。

秦俑丰富而生动地塑造了多种具有一定特点的人物形象。其风格浑厚、洗练，富于感人的艺术魅力，是中国古代塑造艺术臻于成熟的标志。它既继承了战国以来中国的陶塑传统，又为唐代塑造艺术的繁荣奠定了基础，起着承上启下的作用，被誉为“世界第八大奇迹”“人类古代精神文明的瑰宝”。

house, a three-dimensional military book of the Qin Dynasty, but also a brilliant art palace.

The layout of the Terracotta Warriors truly simulates the gathering of the troops of the Qin Dynasty, which also makes these artistic works appear flesh and blood, with personality and emotion. One by one, the terracotta figures are tall in shape, harmonious in proportion, lifelike and one-of-a-kind in expression and some soldiers even wear smiles; their hairs are clear, and their fingers are vivid. They, standing or kneeling, or leading a horse or pressing a sword, are dignified and brave.

Terracotta Warriors have shaped a variety of rich and vivid characters with certain personality. Its refined and mighty style as well as touching artistic charm marks the maturity of ancient Chinese moulding art. It not only inherits the ceramic tradition of China since the Warring States Period, but also lays the foundation for the prosperity of moulding art of the Tang Dynasty. It plays a connecting role and is honored as "the eighth wonder in the world" and "the treasure of ancient human spiritual civilization".

特殊的地理环境，造就了陕西集水乡泽国、平原沃野和高原沟峁于一体的景象。为了保护自然环境，陕西坚持绿色发展，树立和践行“绿水青山就是金山银山”的理念，让三秦大地天更蓝、山更绿、水更清。

The distinctive geographical features of Shaanxi Province have created a landscape where fertile plains and hilly plateaus are integrated with southern water towns. In order to protect the natural environment, Shaanxi adheres to green development, establishes and practices the concept of "lucid waters and lush mountains are invaluable assets", and endeavors to make Shaanxi an even more beautiful place.

Chapter Two

第二篇

青山绿水，持续发展

林间新绿一重重

Lush Mountains and Lucid Waters for Sustainable Development

New Green Leaves Throbbing
Among Branches

国土增绿

Land Greening

生态优先、绿色发展，是站在中华民族永续发展的战略高度提出的理念，也是立足当前满足人民对优美生态环境需

Ecological priority and green development are concepts generated from the strategic height of sustainable development of the Chinese nation, and they are also practical choices in meeting the current needs of the people for a beautiful ecological environment. Shaanxi's ecological environment protection is crucial not only to its own high–quality development, but also to the overall development of the country.

From the concept that "lucid waters and lush mountains are invaluable assets" to the ideology that "if we do not fail Nature, Nature shall never fail us", Shaanxi has become more confident in its commitment to green development and has made

汉中勉县高山茶园

要的现实选择。陕西生态环境保护不仅关乎自身高质量发展，也关乎国家发展大局。

从“绿水青山就是金山银山”到“人不负青山，青山定不负人”，陕西坚持绿色发展的思路愈发清晰，生态保护的成效愈加显著。

在荒漠化治理方面，陕西成为全国第一个完全“拴牢”流动沙地的省份。黄河沿线 860 万亩流动沙地得到固定或半固定，风沙危害得到控制，

significant achievements in ecological protection.

In desertification control, Shaanxi has become the first province in China to have completely stabilized the mobile sandy land. Altogether 8.6 million *mu* (5,733.62 km^2) of mobile sandy land along the Yellow River has been fixed or semi-fixed, and the hazards of sandstorms have been controlled. Desertification control has extended 400 kilometers of Shaanxi's green territory to the north, creating a green miracle of China and even of the whole world.

荒漠化治理使陕西绿色版图向北推进了 400 千米，创造出属于中国乃至世界的绿色奇迹。

在退耕还林还草方面，陕西是退耕还林还草的策源地，也是全国退耕还林成果最显著的省份之一。自 1999 年以来，陕西省累计完成退耕还林还草 4130.64 万亩，完成人工造林 225 万亩、飞播造林 29.4 万亩，治理沙化土地 107.05 万亩，义务植树 8010 万株。

Besides, Shaanxi is the first province and one of the best provinces in China to initiate the strategy of returning the farmland to forestry and the grassland. Since 1999, a total of 41.3064 million *mu* （27,551.37 km^2）of farmland has been returned to forestry and grassland. 2.25 million *mu*（1,507.5 km^2） of artificial afforestation and 294,000 *mu*（196.98 km^2）of aerial afforestation have been completed. Moreover, 1.0705 million *mu*（713.67 km^2）of sandy land has been brought under control, and 80.1 million trees have been planted by volunteers.

In terms of wetland protection, Shaanxi is rich in wetland resources. The wetland covers a total area of 308,500 hectares, including four categories and 12 types, such as river wetland, lake wetland, marsh wetland and constructed wetland, among which river wetland accounts for 83.50% of the total wetland area of the province.

洽川风景区

在湿地保护方面，陕西省湿地资源丰富，湿地总面积 30.85 万公顷，湿地类型包括河流湿地、湖泊湿地、沼泽湿地和人工湿地等 4 大类 12 个湿地类型，其中河流湿地占全省湿地总面积的 83.50%。

在水土保持方面，陕西省水土保持生态修复全国领先。累计治理水土流失面积 8.16 万平方千米，建成淤地坝 3.4 万座，占全国淤地坝总数的 58%。

如今，俯瞰三秦，一幅充溢着绿意的壮美画卷，从北到南绵延千里。榆林绿、延安绿、关中绿、秦巴绿，构成全域绿色的陕西。

In terms of soil and water conservation, Shaanxi Province leads the country in achieving ecological restoration. A total of 81,600 km^2 of soil erosion has been brought under control, and 34,000 silt dams have been built, accounting for 58% of the total in China.

Today, overlooking Shaanxi Province, a magnificent picture decorated with green stretches thousands of miles from Northern to Southern Shaanxi. The green environment pervades in Yulin, Yan'an, the Guanzhong Plain, Qinling-Daba Mountain Range, and the rest of whole Shaanxi Province.

生物保护 Biological Conservation

随着陕西生物多样性保护体系不断完善，管理水平不断提高，生物多样性保护成效不断显现，陕西省 90% 以上的野生动植物物种得到保护。

目前，陕西省分布有野生脊椎动物 931 种；以大熊猫、羚牛、金丝猴和朱鹮为代表的国家重点保护野生动物共计

Shaanxi's unremitting efforts in perfecting the management and protection system of biodiversity are generating more and more effects. More than 90% of the province's wild animal and plant species are under protection.

At present, Shaanxi boasts 931 species of wild vertebrates, 159 species of wild animals and birds under state key protection, including 37 species under State Level I protection and 122 species under State Level II

大熊猫

金丝猴

羚牛

朱鹮

159 种，其中国家 Ⅰ 级保护野生动物 37 种，Ⅱ 级保护野生动物 122 种；省级保护动物 52 种。有种子植物 4600 余种，中药材 3291 种；国家和地方重点保护野生植物为 212 种。

生物多样性保护取得积极进展，陕西省生物多样性实现恢复性增长。秦岭红豆杉、珙桐、独叶草、华山新麦草、太白红杉等珍稀濒危野生植物得到有效保护；野生蕙兰种群分布扩大到秦岭北麓；陕西羽叶报春时隔 100

protection, represented by giant panda, takin, golden monkey and crested ibis. There are 52 species of provincial-level protected animals, more than 4,600 species of seed plants, 3,291 species of Chinese medicinal materials, and 212 species of wild plants under state and local key protection.

Biodiversity protection has made positive progress, and the province's biodiversity has achieved restorative growth. Rare and endangered wild plants, such as Qinling Taxus Chinensis, Davidia Involucrata, Kingdonia Uniflora, Ppsathyrostachys Huashanica, and Larix Chinensis have been effectively protected. The distribution of wild Cymbidium Hybridum has expanded to the northern foot of the Qinling Mountains. Primula Filchnerae Knuth was rediscovered in Yangxian County in 2015, a period of over a century since its last discovery. Kingdonia Uniflora, a first class state key protected wild plant, known as a "natural indicator" of an excellent ecological environment, was first discovered in June 2021 at a

秦岭雨蛙

多年，于2015年在陕西洋县被重新发现。有着优异生态环境“天然指示器”之称的国家一级重点保护野生植物独叶草，于2021年6月在秦岭太白山海拔2700米以下区域被首次发现。

秦岭大熊猫野外种群数量增幅、密度、DNA调查获取率，秦岭人工繁育林麝存栏数量均为全国第一。朱鹮被国际鸟类保护联盟誉为“世界拯救濒危物种的成功典范”。延安子午岭林区的华北豹种群是国内发现数量最大和密度最高的豹种群。开展秦岭细鳞鲑人工驯养、繁育和增殖放流，野生资源得到逐步恢复。

place below the altitude of 2,700 meters of Taibai Mountain in the Qinling Mountains.

Shaanxi ranked first in China in terms of the number increase, density, and DNA acquisition rate of wild population of giant panda, and the number of musk deer in artificial breeding forests in Qinling Mountains. The crested ibis is known as "a successful example of saving endangered species in the world" by the International Union for the Conservation of Birds. The population of North China Leopard in Ziwuling forestry area of Yan'an is also the largest leopard population with the highest density found in China. Work has been done in raising, breeding, proliferating and release of Brachymystax Lenok Tsinlingensis in Qinling Mountains. Wild resources have been gradually restored.

羽叶报春

河流与湿地

Rivers and Wetlands

陕西省切实加大黄河流域生态环境保护力度和高质量发展工作。对标国家《纲要》制定陕西省规划，严格执行污水综合排放标准，加强水功能区限制纳污红线管理。

2021 年，黄河流域生态空间治理十大行动持续开展。黄河粗泥沙拦沙工程全面启动，河湖“清四乱”扎实推进。干流 105 个问题排污口完成整治，渭河入黄断面水质连续两年为优。汉江、丹江出境断面水质持续保持在Ⅱ类，陕南硫铁矿污染专项整治深入开展，南水北调中线工程水源地安全稳定。

渭河是黄河最大的支流，从西向东贯穿陕西全境。从 2012 年开

Shaanxi Province adopted solid measures to strengthen the protection of ecological environment in the Yellow River basin and promote high-quality development. In line with the national "Overall Plan", the plan for Shaanxi Province has been worked out for strict implementation of the overall standards for waste water discharge, and for taking tough hands in setting alarm line for pollution in water function zones.

In 2021, ten actions for ecological spatial governance in the Yellow River basin continued to be carried out. The coarse sediment detention project of the Yellow River has been fully launched, and the clearing of four illegal and excess use of rivers and lakes has been solidly promoted. 105 problem sewage outlets in the main streams have been renovated, and the water quality of the section into the Yellow River of the Weihe River has been excellent for two consecutive years. The water quality at the exit

汉江汉中城市段

始，陕西逐步实现了渭河变清的目标，渭河出境水质为优。如今渭河面貌焕然一新，渭河生态走廊已经成为沿线居民休闲娱乐的好去处。

陕南是南水北调中线工程重要的水源地，占有北上调水总量的70%以上。为了长久保障南水北调中线工程水源地高标准水质，陕西精心呵护水源地，为此实施了大规模的水土保持生态保护和治理工程，先后启动实施了汉江、丹江综合整治，在沿线实施生态环境治理、水资源配置和防洪设施一体化建设工程，根治流域洪涝频发、水土流失严重、水生态恶化等问题。促进迁出地生态恢复进程，水源涵养功能明显改善，实现了

sections of Hanjiang River and Danjiang River has remained at Class II. The special rectification of pyrite pollution in southern Shaanxi has been carried out in depth, and the water source in the middle route of South-to-North Water Transfer remains safe and stable.

As the biggest branch of the Yellow River, the Weihe River winds its way eastward through Shaanxi. From 2012, Shaanxi has gradually reached the goal of making the water in the Weihe River clean again. The trans-provincial water of the Weihe River reaches high quality. Weihe River Ecological Corridor has become a leisure and relaxation resort for nearby residents.

Southern Shaanxi is an important water source for the middle route of the South-to-North Water Diversion Project, accounting for over 70% of water transferred to China's North. In order to ensure long-term high standard water quality of water source for the middle route of the Project, Shaanxi has protected the water source areas with meticulous care, and has carried out a large-scale ecological protection and control project of soil and water conservation. The comprehensive improvement of Hanjiang River and Danjiang River has been launched successively, and the integrated construction projects of ecological environment control,

“一江清水供京津”的目标。

陕西省湿地生物多样性丰富，特别是水鸟种类多，数量大，保护级别高。陕西省共有湿地鸟类 9 目 24 科 121 种，其中属国家一级保护 7 种、二级保护 12 种，省级重点保护 19 种。国家二级保护野生植物 1 种，省级重点保护野生植物

water resources allocation and flood control facilities have been implemented along the rivers, so as to solve the problems of frequent flood and waterlogging, serious soil erosion and water ecological deterioration. The ecological restoration project of the water source has been enhanced, with the function of water conservation significantly improved. The goal of "supplying Beijing and Tianjin with clean water" has been achieved.

Shaanxi boasts diversified biological resources in wetlands, especially waterfowl with various species, in large numbers, and at high protection levels. There are a total of 121 species of wetland birds belonging to nine orders and 24 families in

2种。

目前，陕西共建立各级湿地类型自然保护区9处，国家湿地公园（试点）43处，其中，26处通过国家验收，初步形成了以国家公园为主体、自然保护地为基础、各类自然公园为补充的自然保护地分类体系。

Shaanxi, of which 7 species are under national first-class protection, 12 under national second-class protection, and 19 under provincial level protection. One specie of wild plants is under national second-class protection, and two species are under provincial key protection.

At present, Shaanxi has established 9 wetland natural reserves at various levels and 43 national wetland parks (pilots), of which 26 have passed the national inspection. A natural reserve classification system has been preliminarily formed with national parks as the main body, natural reserves as the foundation, and natural parks of various types as supplementary.

陕西潼关黄河国家湿地公园

沿黄公路
——中国的“一号公路”

Yanhuang Highway: China's "Highway One"

陕西沿黄公路是陕西省沿黄河西岸修建的一条南北布线的省级公路，北起榆林市府谷县墙头乡，南至渭南市华山脚下的莲花座，全长800余千米，沿线经过榆林市、延安市、韩城市、渭南市等4市12区（县）。

沿黄公路于2017年8月底正式建成通车。随着沿黄公路的通车，一条兼具生态、观光、旅游、文化、城镇发展诸多功能的经济带也将

Yanhuang Highway (also Shaanxi Yanhuang Sightseeing Highway), a north-south provincial highway built along the west bank of the Yellow River in Shaanxi Province, stretches over 800 kilometers from Qiangtou Township in Fugu County, Yulin City in the north to Lotus Seat Statue at the foot of Huashan Mountain in Weinan City in the south, passing 12 districts and counties in 4 cities including Yulin, Yan'an, Hancheng and Weinan.

As the highway officially opened to traffic at the end of August 2017, a multifunctional economic belt is being formed encompassing ecology, sightseeing, tourism, culture and urban development.

形成。

沿黄公路沿途珠链般串起了府谷古城、香炉寺、白云山、吴堡古城、文安驿古镇、乾坤湾、延安、壶口瀑布、黄河龙门、党家村、司马迁祠、洽川湿地、丰图义仓、潼关古城、西岳华山等50余处名胜古迹景点。它因为高颜值而被广大自驾爱好者称为中国的“一号公路”。

沿黄公路连接9条高速公路、13条国省干线公路以及80条县乡公路，完善优化了陕北和关中东部地区路网结构，为陕西省路网增添了一条新的交通主动脉，对陕北能源化工基地、沿黄特色农业基地的建设，沿黄旅游开发、生态环境保护、区域经济合作、特困地区脱贫以及防汛应急抢险等起到积极促进作用。

Like a pearl necklace, Yanhuang Highway strings more than 50 famous scenic spots and historical sites, including Fugu Ancient City, Xianglu Temple, Baiyun Mountain, Wubu Ancient Town, Wenanyi Ancient Town, Qiankun Bay, Yan'an City, the Hukou Waterfall, Longmen of the Yellow River, Dang's Village, Sima Qian Temple, Hechuan Wetland, Fengtu Granary, Tongguan Ancient City, and Huashan Mountain. Because of the gorgeous view along the road, Yanhuang Highway has soon become China's "Highway One" to self-driving enthusiasts.

Yanhuang Highway links 9 expressways, 13 national and provincial main highways and 80 county and township roads, optimizing the road network structure in northern Shaanxi and eastern Guanzhong area and adding a new traffic artery to the road network of Shaanxi Province. At the same time, it is expected to promote the development of energy and chemical bases in northern Shaanxi, special agricultural bases along the Yellow River, tourism development, ecological environmental protection, and regional economic cooperation along the Yellow River, poverty alleviation in areas of dire poor, flood control, emergency and rescue services.

沿黄公路

2021年，陕西紧紧围绕谱写陕西高质量发展新篇章目标，统筹推进疫情防控和经济社会发展，扎实做好"六稳"工作，全面落实"六保"任务，勠力同心、顽强拼搏，全年经济呈现持续恢复、结构向善、动能蓄积、质效提升的良好态势，高质量发展取得新成效，实现了"十四五"良好开局。2021年，陕西省实现地区生产总值29800.98亿元，按不变价格计算，比上年增长6.5%。

In 2021, with the goal of writing a new chapter in the high-quality development of Shaanxi as the center, Shaanxi made coordinated efforts in promoting Covid-19 control and social and economic development. Shaanxi strove to ensure stability on six fronts and maintain security in six areas. With joint hands and tenacious efforts, Shaanxi's economic development has been maintaining a sound momentum in sustained economic recovery, improving structure, accumulating kinetic energy and improving quality and efficiency. The high-quality development has witnessed new achievements. Shaanxi made a good start in the first year of the 14th Five-Year Plan. In 2021, Shaanxi's GDP reached 298.0098 billion yuan, which is a 6.5% increase at constant price as compared with that of last year.

Chapter Three

第三篇

蓬勃生机，开拓进取

晴空一鹤排云上

Booming with Vitality and Forging Ahead

A Crane Flapping Its Wings
to the Clear Sky

发展潜力
Development Potential

1. 工业生产保持增长
Industrial Production Keeping Growing

2021 年，陕西省规模以上工业增加值比上年增长 7.6%，工业新增产能项目释放产值 1000 亿元。

In 2021, the added value of industries above the designated size in the province has increased by 7.6% over the previous year, and the output value of new industrial capacity projects has reached 100 billion yuan.

西安高新区

中航西安飞机工业集团生产的运 -20 飞机

装备制造业是陕西的支柱产业，已形成了门类较为齐全、具有相当规模和水平的装备制造业体系。2021 年，陕西围绕构建数控机床、光子、航空等 23 条重点产业链实施的一大批项目进展顺利，

The equipment manufacturing industry is Shaanxi's pillar industry, and an equipment manufacturing system has been formed with a relatively complete range of categories and a considerable scale and level. The year 2021 has witness successful implementation of a large number of projects centering on 23 key industrial chains, including CNC machine tools, photonics, aviation, etc. Some projects were put into

比亚迪新能源汽车

三星闪存芯片二期、奕斯伟硅产业基地、西安吉利汽车、彩虹光电扩产技改等项目正式投产，隆基 15 吉瓦高效单晶电池、比亚迪高端智能终端产业园、中兴科创园等项目加快建设。

operation, including Samsung Flash Memory Chip (Phase II), ESWin Silicon Industrial Base, Xi'an Geely Automobile, Caihong Optoelectronics Production Expansion and Technical Transformation. Projects were accelerating their construction, including Longji 15 GW High Efficiency Single Crystal Battery, BYD Up-scale Intelligent Terminal Industrial Park and ZTE Science and Technology Innovation Park.

2. 创新创造潜能加速释放

Accelerating the Release of Innovation and Creative Potential

2021 年陕西举全省之力推进秦创原创新驱动总平台建设，制定实施三年行动计划和“1+N”政策体系，设立规模 20 亿元的科创母基金，常态化举办路演活动 130 多场，115 项科技成果落地

In 2021, Shaanxi took the whole province's efforts to promote the construction of Qinchuangyuan Innovation-driven Platform, formulated and implemented the three-year action plan and "1+N" policy system, established a science and innovation master fund of 2 billion yuan, and held more than 130 routine roadshows. 115 scientific and technological achievements were transformed and registered as enterprises. The number of scientific and technological small and

转化并注册企业，科技型中小企业增长 38.67%，高新技术企业增长 35.48%，技术合同成交额增长 33.23%。

着力夯实创新基础，加强知识产权保护，16 家共性技术研发平台和创新联合体投入运营，空天动力陕西实验室启动建设，国家超算西安中心、中国—中亚“一带一路”

medium-sized enterprises increased by 38.67%, and the number of high-tech enterprises increased by 35.48%. The turnover of technology contracts increased by 33.23%.

Great efforts were made to lay solid foundation for innovation and to strengthen intellectual property protection.16 generic technology research and development platforms and innovation consortiums were launched. The construction of Aerospace and Astronautics Propulsion Shaanxi Laboratory was launched, and the National Supercomputing Center (Xi'an) and the Belt and Road Joint Laboratory of China-Central Asia were successfully approved. 26 scientific and technological achievements

智能搬运机器人在隆基单晶硅太阳能电池工厂内工作

“嫦娥五号”上升器、返回器实验室

联合实验室等顺利获批，26 项科技成果获国家科学技术奖。发挥企业创新主体作用，规模以上工业企业研发活动覆盖率、研发投入强度增幅超过前四年总和。

received the national science and technology award. The leading position of enterprises were given full play in innovation. The research and development activity coverage, as well as investment intensity of industrial enterprises above designated size has increased by more than the sum of the previous four years.

3. 战略性新兴产业总体发展向好

Overall Growth of Strategic Emerging Industries Moving Towards Better

陕西深入推进供给侧结构性改革，沉着有力应对各种风险挑战，战略性新兴产业规模不断扩大，效益不断提升，引领带动作用凸显，已成为陕西实现经济高质量发展的生力军和“新支柱”。

陕西积极抢抓全球新科技革命、产业变革等重大机遇，充分发挥人才、技术、产业和环境等优势，战略性新兴产业快速发展。随着经济结构优化升级，战略性新兴产业发展速度快于 GDP 增速，市场化特征明显，活力、效益较为显著，已逐步发展成为全省经济的重要支柱产业，对经济贡献明显。

陕西持续培育壮大战略性新兴产业，战略性新兴产业各具特色、亮点纷呈，新一代信息技术、生物、新能源、数字创意产业等四大产业成为引领经济发展的新引擎。

Shaanxi further promoted supply-side structural reform, and responded with calm and effectiveness to various risks and challenges. With their increasingly expanding scale and rising benefits, the strategic emerging industries are displaying their leading role, and have become a new force and "new pillar" in promoting Shaanxi's achieving high-quality economic development.

Shaanxi took the initiative in grabbing the great opportunities of the global new science and technology revolution and industrial transformation, and in putting into full play the advantages of talents, technology, industry and environment, and has achieved rapid progress in the strategic emerging industries. With the optimization and upgrading of the economic structure, the strategic emerging industries are developing at a faster speed than that of GDP growth. Along with their sharp market-oriented characteristics and outstanding vitality and efficiency, they have gradually become important pillar industries, and have made significant contribution to Shaanxi's economy.

Shaanxi has been continuously cultivating and fostering strategic emerging industries. The strategic emerging industries enjoy distinctive features and advantages. The new generation of four industries, including information technology, biology, new energy and digital creative industry, have become new engines in leading the economic development.

特色产业
Specialty Industries

1. "3+X" 农业特色产业
"3+X" Agricultural Specialty Industries

乡村振兴，产业兴旺是关键。2021 年陕西省深入推进乳制品、苹果、茶叶、猕猴桃等 9 个农业全产业链建设，促进农村一、二、三产业融合发展，加大金融服务农业产业化力度，培育发展家庭农场、农民合作社和农业社会化服务组织，不断壮

风景如画的汉中市宁强茶园

大“3+X”特色产业规模，引导创建5个国家级、30个省级农村产业融合示范园。

近年来，陕西依托资源禀赋，扎实推进农业特色产业“3+X”工程。“3”即大力发展以千亿级苹果为代表的果业、以千亿级奶山羊为代表的畜牧业、以千亿级棚室栽培为代表的设施农业；

Industrial prosperity is essential to rural revitalization. Shaanxi Province efforts should be exerted in further promoting the construction of 9 agriculture industry chains, including dairy products, apple, tea, and kiwifruit. Besides, further work will be exerted in facilitating the integration and development of the first, the second, and the third industries in the rural areas, stepping up efforts in providing financial services for the industrialization of agriculture. Shaanxi will develop family farms, farmers cooperatives and agricultural socialized service organizations to expand the scale of "3+X" agricultural special industries. In addition, Shaanxi will guide the establishment of 5 state-level and

"X"即因地制宜做优做强魔芋、中药材、核桃、红枣和有机、富硒、林特系列产品等区域特色产业。

目前，陕西已经建成黄土高原千万亩集中优势苹果产业带，产量超千万吨；建成世界最大的秦岭北麓猕猴桃集中产区，产量占世界近 1/3。陕西的奶山羊目前已经成为世界上最大的奶山羊群体，羊乳制品占国内市场份额的 85%，产销量稳居全国第一。陕西成为全国最大的奶山羊养殖基地、羊乳加工基地，全省 12.3 万余户 31.4 万人在奶山羊产业链上，持续带动农民增收致富。陕西设施农业规模居全国第六、西北首位，反季节蔬菜省内自给率提高到 70% 以上。"X"区域特色产业形成了"小板块、大聚集""小产业、广覆盖"格局，茶叶已成为陕南农民增收的支柱产业，魔芋、木耳等产业也快速发展，有力地促进了产业脱贫和农民增收。

30 provincial-level rural industrial integration demonstration parks.

With its rich resource endowment, Shaanxi has made solid progress in promoting the "3+X" Agricultural Specialty Industries in recent years. "3" refers to vigorous development of three industries, including the fruit industry represented by apples, the animal husbandry represented by dairy goats, and the facility agriculture represented by greenhouse cultivation, all of which are of hundreds of billions output value. "X" means making local specialty industries better and stronger in line with local conditions, such as konjac, Chinese medicinal materials, walnuts, red dates, and organic, selenium-enriched and forest-related products.

Up to now, an advantageous industrial belt of apples covering ten million mu has been formed on the Loess Plateau, with a total apple output of over tens of millions of tons. As for kiwifruit, the world's largest production area has been built at the northern foot of the Qinling Mountains, accounting for almost 1/3 of the world's total. Shaanxi boasts the largest number of dairy goats in stock in the world. The amount of goat dairy products takes up 85% of the domestic market share, ranking first in terms of the production and sale volumes in China. Shaanxi has the largest dairy goat breeding base and goat milk processing base in China, attracting 314,000 people from 123,000 families to work in this dairy goat industry chain, providing sustained impetus in increasing farmers' income and making them get rich. The facility agriculture in Shaanxi Province ranks sixth in the country and first in the Northwestern China in scale. As such, the province's self-sufficiency rate of off-season vegetables rose to 70%. Shaanxi's local specialty "X" industries have formed a pattern of "small sectors with large clusters" and "small industries with wide coverage". The tea industry is now a pillar for farmers in Southern Shaanxi to increase their income, along with the rapid development in konjac and agaric industries. All these have made great contributions to getting locals out of poverty and increasing farmers' income.

兴平市庄头镇的金银花特色产业

2. 文化旅游产业 Cultural Tourism

2021 年，陕西面对文旅发展的新形势、新特征，把握新发展阶段，贯彻新发展理念，构建新发展格局，统筹抓好常态化疫情防控与文旅工作，全年安排文化事业发展资金 3.72 亿元；新建、在建文旅重大项目 139 个，总投资额 2823.46 亿元；接待国内旅游者 3.91 亿人次，旅游总收入 3433.95 亿元，同比分别增长 9.40%、24.31%，交出了“十四五”开局起步亮丽成绩单。

In 2021, facing the new situation and new features of cultural tourism development, Shaanxi understood the new development stage, applied the new development philosophy, and created a new development dynamic. Shaanxi coordinated routine Covid-19 control and cultural tourism, and allocated 372 million yuan for the development of cultural undertakings throughout the year. 139 major cultural tourism projects have been built or are under construction, with a total investment of 282.346 billion yuan. Altogether 391 million domestic tourists were received, with a total tourism revenue of 343.395 billion yuan, up 9.40% and 24.31% year-on-year respectively, making a brilliant start in the 14th Five-Year Plan.

西安华商传媒文化产业园

西安“蓝海风·漫巷”书店主题商业综合体

围绕庆祝建党100周年创作了碗碗腔《骄杨之恋》、秦腔《织梦人》、杂技剧《战魂》、秦腔组曲《根据地》、历史组歌《照金》等一批优秀现实主义精品剧目。话剧《共产党宣言》《路遥》《平凡的世界》全国巡演百余场，“陕派话剧”享誉全国。电视剧《号手就位》《逐梦蓝天》、电影《凿空者》、纪录片《千年陕菜》等登陆央视，电影《柳青》等在全国上映，《国家至上》《红箭红箭》等多部广播剧在央广播出，文艺精品不断涌现，文化影响力持续提升。

In celebrating the 100th anniversary of the founding of the CPC, a number of excellent realistic works have been created, including the Bowl Opera Yang Kaihui, the Qin Opera Dream Weavers, the acrobatic drama War Soul, the Qin Opera Suite Base, and the historical suite Zhao Jin. The dramas The Communist Manifesto, Lu Yao and World of Plainness have toured more than 100 times in China, and "Shaanxi Drama" enjoys a national reputation. TV series such as The Glory of Youth, Dream in The Blue Sky, the movie The Pioneer and the documentary A Thousand Years of Shaanxi Cuisine have been aired on CCTV; films such as Liu Qing have been screened across the country; and a number of radio dramas such as The State Comes First and Red Arrows have been broadcast on CCTV.

4 research projects featuring the Yellow River culture were approved by the Ministry of Culture and Tourism. 13

4 项黄河文化研究课题获文化和旅游部立项，“张骞传说”等 13 个项目入选第五批国家级非遗名录，“视频直播家乡年”活动受到文化和旅游部通报表扬。在“文化和自然遗产日”系列活动中，为国家重点扶持的 12 家非遗就业工坊集中授牌，组织 288 项非遗项目、412类非遗产品进行线上线下展示销售，让非遗文化更多地融入现代生活，得到更深层次发展。

改造提升全省智慧旅游综合服务平台，成功申报文化和旅游部“民歌智能计算与服务技术重点实验室”，立项国家文旅科技创新项目 3 个，建成全省“5G+ 文旅”示范应用场景 6 个、智慧旅游项目 2 个，数字赋能效应显著增强。

projects, including "Legend of Zhang Qian", were selected into the fifth batch of National Intangible Cultural Heritage list, and the "Live Video Show of Spring Festival in My Hometown" was praised by the Ministry of Culture and Tourism. Among the "Cultural and Natural Heritage Day" activities, 12 key state-supported intangible cultural heritage workshops were conferred nameplates, and 288 items of intangible cultural heritage projects and 412 categories of intangible cultural heritage products were displayed and sold online and offline, enabling intangible cultural heritage to be more integrated into modern life and achieve further development.

The Smart Tourism Comprehensive Service Platform in Shaanxi was transformed and upgraded, and "the Key Laboratory of Folk Song Intelligent Computing and Service Technology" was successfully approved by the Ministry of Culture and Tourism. Besides, 3 national culture and tourism science and technology innovation projects were established, and 6 "5G + cultural tourism" demonstration application scenarios and 2 smart tourism projects were built in the province. The digital empowerment effect was significantly enhanced.

汉中市勉县风光

第九届陕西省艺术节展览在宝鸡美术馆举办

经济布局
Specialty Industries

1. 加快构建现代产业体系
Accelerating the Establishment of Modern Industry System

认真落实国家关于振作工业经济运行，推动工业高质量发展的实施方案，加快集成电路、新能源汽车、新型显示等重点产业

西安高新技术产业开发区

Shaanxi conscientiously carried out the national implementation plan of invigorating the operation of industrial economy and promoting high-quality development, and accelerated innovation and development of key industries, such as integrated circuit, new energy vehicle, and advanced display. With the chain leadership system as the crux, efforts were exerted in promoting the continuation, supplementation and strengthening of 23 key industrial chains. The policy support was strengthened in the application of first sets and first batches of key equipment. The promotion scheme of key industrial chains of energy and chemical industries was carried out, along with the advancing of

创新发展。以链长制为抓手推进 23 条重点产业链延链补链强链，加大“首台套”“首批次”应用政策支持力度。落实能源化工重点产业链推进方案，推动

the construction of Yulin Energy Revolution Innovation Demonstration Zone. Further integration was pushed in modern service industry, advanced manufacturing industry, and modern agriculture. In addition, Shaanxi also made efforts in

榆林能源革命创新示范区建设。推动现代服务业和先进制造业、现代农业深度融合，促进服务业聚集区公共服务平台提质增效。推动数字产业化、产业数字化。

improving the quality and efficiency of public service platform in service industry clusters, as well as the digital industrialization and industrial digitalization.

新能源项目

2. 外贸外资保持稳定增长势头
Steady Growth in Foreign Trade and Investment

2021年，陕西外贸表现出色，进出口规模均创历史同期新高。面对严峻复杂的全球经贸环境，陕西于变局中谋新局，进出口总值突破4000亿元大关，达4757.8亿元人民币，同比增长25.9%，交出了有外贸进出口统计以来最亮眼的一张答卷。

2021年陕西加快推进中欧班列（西安）集结中心建设，开通日韩过境货物测试班列，长

The year 2021 has witnessed impressive achievements of Shaanxi in its foreign trade, with the imports and exports volumes both hitting a record high for that period in history. In the face of the serious and complex global economic and trade situation, Shaanxi has sought new strategies in the changing situation. the total value of import and export exceeded 400 billion yuan and reached 475.78 billion yuan, which was a year-on-year increase of 25.9%, coming as the most outstanding achievement ever recorded.

In 2021, Shaanxi sped up the construction of Xi'an Assembly Center of China-Europe Railway Express (Xi'an), and launched the first trial run for Japan-South Korea transit cargo train services. The core indicators of Chang'an Express held the leading position in China. Xixian Airport Comprehensive Bonded Zone and Baoji Comprehensive

第七届丝绸之路国际艺术节：用舞台记录时代

安号核心指标稳居全国前列，西咸空港、宝鸡综保区封关运营，关中综保区通过正式验收。上合组织农业技术交流培训示范基地实质性运行，陕西国际贸易“单一窗口”展示大厅和金融服务平台建成，自贸区 8 项创新经验在全国复制推广。丝博会、农高会、欧亚经济论坛等重大经贸活动成功举办。开放招商取得新成效，陕西省新设外商投资企业 312 家，同比增长 12.23%；实际利用外资 102.46 亿美元，同比增长 21.35%。

Bonded Zone have started to put into operation, and Guanzhong Comprehensive Bonded Zone has passed the national inspection. The SCO Agricultural Technology Exchange and Training Demonstration Base was put into use. Shaanxi International Trade "Single Window" Exhibition Hall and the Financial Service Platform have also been built. 8 innovation achievements of the Free Trade Area have been copied and promoted nationwide. Major economic and trade events such as the Silk Expo, the China Yangling Agricultural Hi-Tech Fair (CAF), and the Euro-Asia Economic Forum were successfully held. New achievements were made in opening up and attracting investment. 312 new foreign-invested enterprises were established in Shaanxi, a year-on-year increase of 12.23%. Actual utilization of foreign capital reached $10.246 billion, a year-on-year increase of 21.35%.

西安港

3. 协调发展成效逐步显现
Gradual Achievements in the Coordinated Development

陕西省落实新时代推动西部大开发形成新格局若干措施，加快完善经济发展布局；推广“总部＋基地”“研发＋生产”“飞地经济”等模式，推动三大区域协调发展；制定

Shaanxi made efforts in implementing several measures in promoting the West Development to form a new pattern in the new era, and in accelerating the perfection of economic development layout. The modes of "Headquarters + Base", "Research and Development + Production", and Enclave Economy were further popularized to advance the coordinated development of the three major fields. The implementation plan was worked out for the development

十天高速与安石二级公路池河段

关中平原城市群建设“十四五”实施方案、呼包鄂榆城市群建设“十四五”重点合作事项，编制西安都市圈发展规划，加快西安—咸阳一体化发展进程，推动城市群高质量发展。

of urban agglomeration in Guanzhong Plain in the 14th Five-Year Plan, and the key cooperation matters of urban agglomeration of Hohhot, Baotou, Erdos and Yulin in the 14th Five-Year Plan. In addition, Shaanxi has drawn up the development plan for the development of Xi'an metropolitan area to accelerate the integration of Xi'an and Xianyang, and promote high-quality development of urban agglomeration.

秦创原

Qinchuangyuan

科技是国之利器，国家赖之以强， 企业赖之以赢，人民生活赖之以好。作为科技大省、人才大省，陕西省科技创新综合实力雄厚，是我国西部地区的创新高地。党的十八大以来，陕西深入学习贯彻习近平总书记来陕考察重要讲话重要指示，扎实落实创新驱动发展战略，不断深化科技体制改革，优化科技创新环境，努力推动科技与经济深度融合，以科技助力陕西经济高质量发展、内涵式发展。

2021 年 3 月，为进一步加速释放创新创造潜能，陕西省高规格启动建设秦创原创新驱动平台（以下简称“秦创原”）。

作为陕西省创新驱动发展总平台和创新驱动发展总源头，秦创原坚持企业主体、人才主力、市场主导、政府主推，以建设立体联动“孵化器”、科技成果产业化“加速器”和两链融合“促进器”为目标，着力打造具

Science and technology are the bedrock upon which a country relies for its strength, enterprises for success, and people for a better life. As a leading province of science and technology and talents, Shaanxi Province is an innovation highland in western China for its strong comprehensive strength in sci-tech innovation. Since the 18th CPC National Congress, Shaanxi has been thoroughly implementing the important speech and instructions of General Secretary Xi Jinping during his inspection of Shaanxi Province, carrying out the innovation-driven development strategy, making unremitting efforts in deepening the reform of the scientific and technological system, optimizing the sci-tech innovation environment, striving to promote the deep integration of science and technology and economy, and making best use of science and technology to facilitate Shaanxi's high-quality and connotative economic development.

In March 2021, Shaanxi launched the project of Qinchuangyuan Innovation Platform (hereafter referred as Qinchuangyuan) to further accelerate the release of innovative and creative potential.

Serving as the general platform and source of innovation-driven development in Shaanxi Province, Qinchuangyuan adheres to the principle of taking enterprises as the main entity, talents as the main force, market as the leading factor and the government as the major initiating role. With the aim of establishing the three-dimensional coordinated "incubators", "accelerators" of the industrialization of scientific and technological achievements, and "promoters" of the integration of the innovation chain and the industry chain, Qinchuangyuan is striving to build a

有鲜明特色和竞争力的高水平平台。

经过一年多建设，秦创原创新驱动平台框架基本形成。总窗口设立规模为20亿元的科创母基金，常态化举办路演活动130多场，116项科技成果落地转化并注册企业，科技型中小企业增长38.6%，高新技术企业增长35.48%，技术合同成交额增长33.2%。高校院所、龙头企业、金融机构快速聚集，一批重大 产业项目和科创平台相继落地。自建成以来，秦创原创新活力持续升温，创新生态持续优化，总窗口作用逐步发挥。

秦创原是陕西依托科技和人才资源推动全省高质量发展的一个缩影。

“十四五”期间，围绕高质量发展，陕西省加快推动科技创新，构建现代产业体系。一系列思路规划全面布局、精准落子，纸面蓝图正一步步变为现实，化作强劲创新引擎，蕴蓄起陕西高质量发 展的强劲动力。

high–level platform with distinctive characteristics and competitiveness.

With over one year's effort, the framework of Qinchuang Innovative Platform has basically taken shape. With a sci–tech innovation master fund of 2 billion yuan for the Main Window, more than 130 routine roadshows have been made, and 16 scientific and technological achievements have been transformed and registered as enterprises. The number of small and medium–sized sci–tech enterprises increased by 38.6%, and the number of high–tech enterprises increased by 35.48%. The turnover of technology contracts increased by 33.2%. Universities, colleges, institutes, leading enterprises and financial institutions have gathered rapidly, and a number of major industrial projects and sci–tech innovation platforms have been launched one after another. Since its completion, with the continuing heating up of its innovation vitality and the sustained optimization of the innovation ecology, Qinchuangyuan is displaying its crucial role with the Main Window.

Qinchuangyuan fully illustrates Shaanxi's efforts in promoting high–quality development based on science and technology and human resources

During the period of 14th Five–Year Plan, Shaanxi will center on high–quality development and accelerate the promotion of sci–tech innovation to construct the modern industry system. A series of ideas are planned with comprehensive layout and precise placement. The paper blueprint is becoming a reality step by step, which will turn into a strong innovation engine and accumulate a strong driving force for the high–quality development of Shaanxi.

2021 年，陕西持之以恒办好惠民安民实事，出台“十四五”促进居民增收推动富民惠民意见和促进城乡居民增收 10 条措施，下达就业补助资金 23.85 亿元，发放稳岗返还资金 16.6 亿元，城镇新增就业 44.56 万人，城镇居民、农村居民人均可支配收入分别增长 7.5%、10.7%。

In 2021, Shaanxi continued its efforts in conducting practical things to benefit people. Altogether 10 suggestions and measures were issued to help residents increase their income and get rich during the 14th Five-Year Plan period. The employment subsidy funds of 2.385 billion yuan were granted, and the employment stability subsidy funds of 1.66 billion yuan were provided. 445,600 new urban jobs were created, with the per capita disposable income of urban and rural residents increasing by 7.5% and 10.7% respectively.

Chapter Four

第四篇

安居乐业，脱贫致富

丰年留客足鸡豚

Living and Working in Peace, Shaking off Poverty and Getting Rich

Ample Food for Guests
in Good Years

便捷出行

Convenient Transportation

2021年，陕西用心用情办好交通运输，更贴近民生实事。坚守为民情怀，致力解决一批群众关心、基层需要、社会关注的热点难点问题。完成农村公路安全生命防护工程5154千米、桥涵配套和危桥改造工程8139延米；6月，西安地铁14号线正式开通运行，目前运营的地铁线路有8条。全

西安三桥立交

In 2021, Shaanxi made great efforts in handling transportation and other matters closely related with people's livelihood. Adhering to the interests of the people, the government was committed to solving a number of hot and difficult issues of public concern, primary needs, and social concern. A total of 5,154 kilometers of the rural road safety projects were completed, in addition to 8,139 linear meters of bridges and culverts maintenance project and unsafe bridge reconstruction project. Xi'an Metro Line 14 was officially put into operation in June, 2021, with altogether 8 metro lines in operation up to now. Over the whole province, 28,000 tourism chartered buses, cross-city coaches, and road transport vehicles for dangerous goods were employed with real-time monitoring

省 2.8 万辆“两客一危”营运车辆实时监测、安全高效运行；新建“司机之家”6 个；推动网约车平台增设“一键叫车”功能，推广巡游车 95128 电召服务，便利老年人打车出行；创建 6 个农村客货邮融合发展样板县（区）；全年 ETC 发行突破 70 万套；道路运输驾驶员从业资格证补发等 5 项高频服务事项实现“跨省通办”。

2021 年，陕西印发《巩固拓展交通脱贫攻坚成果 服务乡村振兴战略实施 助推县域经济高质量发展的实施意见》，建立“两通”动态监测体系，坚决消除“通返不通”隐患。制定《全面做好农村公路“路长制”工作的实施意见》，83 个县

to ensure safe and efficient operation; 6 "Driver Home" sites have been built. To facilitate taxi travel for the elderly, Shaanxi pushed the online car-hailing platform to add a "one-click car-hailing" function. The 95128 roving-car call service was also offered. 6 rural model counties (districts) for integrated development of passenger transport, freight transport, and postal delivery were created. The annual issuance of ETC exceeded 700,000. 5 high-frequency services, including the reissuance of road transport driver certificates, are now available across provinces.

In 2021, Shaanxi issued the Implementation Opinions on Consolidating and Expanding the Achievements of Poverty Alleviation by Transportation to Serve the Implementation of the Rural Revitalization Strategy and Boost High-quality Development of County Economies, while establishing a dynamic monitoring system for the "two access" program (access to tarmac or cement roads and access to bus services), and resolutely eliminating the hidden problems of returning to the inaccessible situation. The Guidelines on Implementing the Road Chief System for Rural Roads was formulated and implemented in 83 counties (districts). Altogether, we have built 2 national "Four Good Rural Road" (good in construction, governance, maintenance,

西安地铁 2 号线

（区）落地实施。创建“四好农村路”全国市域示范创建突出单位 2 个、全国示范县 6 个，省级示范市 2 个、示范县 10 个，全省“最美农村路”10 条。补助 5000 万元支持客车“村村通”常态化运行。新改建完善农村公路 7681 千米，其中 30 户以上自然村通硬化路 3315 千米。推进实施乡村旅游路、资源路、产业路，助推乡村振兴和县域经济发展。

定制客运、旅游客运和商务包车等运输服务新业态在陕西蓬勃发展，不断满足群众个性化、多样化出行需求。“绿巨人”动车组开行，实现 10 个地级市全覆盖。宝鸡市眉县、安康市石泉县列入全国第二批城乡交通运输一体化示范创建县。

and operation) demonstration cities, 6 national demonstration counties, 2 provincial demonstration cities, 10 provincial demonstration counties, and 10 "most beautiful rural roads" in the province. A subsidy of 50 million yuan has been provided to support the regular operation of buses connecting every village. We have upgraded or perfected 7,681 kilometers of rural roads, including 3,315 kilometers of paved roads for unincorporated villages with more than 30 households. Moreover, we have promoted the development of rural tourism, resource and industrial roads to boost rural revitalization and county economic development.

New forms of transport services, such as customized passenger transport, tourist passenger transport and commercial chartered buses, have developed vigorously in Shaanxi, which constantly meets people's personalized and diversified travel needs. The "Green Giant" bullet trains now cover all 10 prefecture-level cities. Mei County of Baoji City and Shiquan County of Ankang City were included in the second batch of demonstration counties for the integration of urban and rural transportation.

西安北车站高铁编组站

民生工程 Livelihood Projects

1. 教育 Education

陕西省教育资源丰厚，共有高等教育学校 110 所（不含 6 所军事院校），其中普通高校 96 所（含独立院校 9 所）、成人高校 14 所。有 8 所高校入选国家“双一流”建设高校，8 所高职院校入选全国“双高计划”建设院校。

2021 年，陕西扎实推进义务教育

Shaanxi Province enjoys rich educational resources. Besides 6 military academies, there are also 110 colleges and universities in Shaanxi, including 96 common ones (with 9 independent colleges) and 14 adult colleges and universities. 8 universities are included on the list of China's "Double First Class" Initiative, with another 8 vocational colleges included on the list of China's "Double High Standards Project".

In 2021, Shaanxi made solid progress in easing the burden of excessive homework and off-campus tutoring for students

西北大学新校区

生动的地理课

“双减”工作，职业教育、高等教育得到加强，新增 3 个学科进入国家新一轮“双一流”建设规划。

undergoing compulsory education. Vocational education and higher education were strengthened, with 3 more disciplines included in the new round national "double first-class" construction plan.

2. 医疗 Medical Care

2021年，陕西省“三医”联动改革不断深化，在全国率先实现城乡基层中医馆全覆盖，药品安全治理能力和保障水平进一步提升。职工基本医疗保险和城

In 2021, the joint reform of medical service, medication and medical assurance was further deepened. Shaanxi took the lead in achieving full coverage of traditional Chinese medicine clinics in the rural and urban areas, with further improvement of the drug safety management and guarantee abilities. Within the scopes of basic medical insurance for

现代化的医院

乡居民基本医疗保险政策范围内住院报销比例分别稳定在 80% 和 70% 左右，大病专项救治病种扩大到 30 种，新冠疫苗接种率达到 86.8%。

employees and urban and rural residents, the proportion of hospitalization reimbursement remained stable at about 80% and 70% respectively; the number of diseases covered by the Special Treatment for Serious Diseases was expanded to 30, and the vaccination rate of Covid-19 vaccine reached 86.8%.

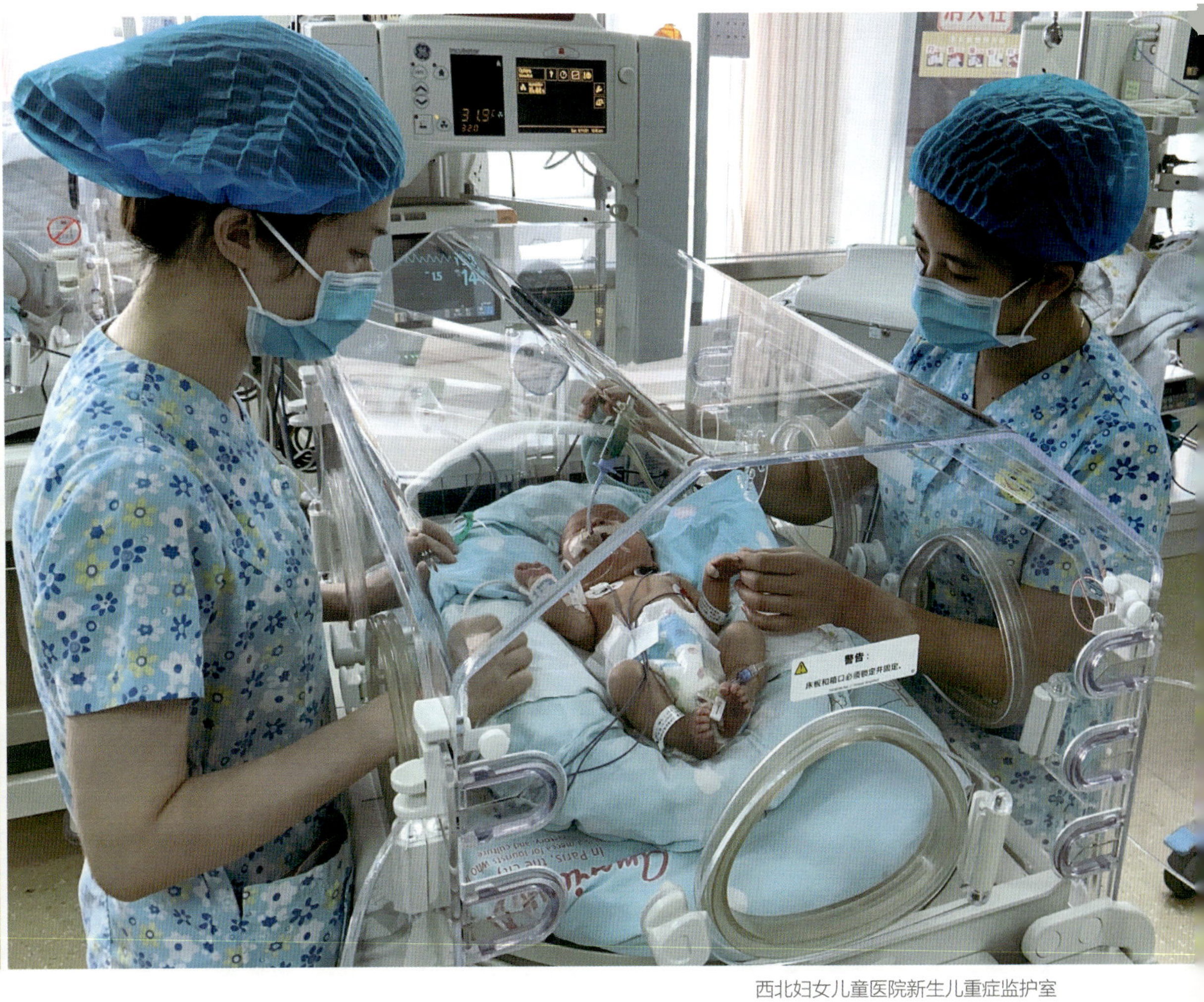

西北妇女儿童医院新生儿重症监护室

3. 住房 Housing

2021 年，陕西聚焦“共同缔造”，不断提升人民群众美好环境与幸福生活；聚焦“房住不炒”，切实促进房地产业良性循环和健康发展；聚焦“住有所居”，切实解决城镇困难群众住房问题。

全省保障性安居工程完成投资 229.64 亿元，棚户区改造新开工 10239 套，基本建成 29815 套，发放城镇住房保障家庭租赁补贴 42687 户，公租房新开工 5068 套，保障性租赁住房新开工 22421 套；城镇老旧小区改造新开工 3634 个，惠及 39.34 万户。

In 2021, Shaanxi focused on the "Joint Construction of Beautiful Environment and Happy Life", and made ceaseless efforts in improving qualities of environment and people's life. By putting emphasis on advocating houses for living in rather than speculative investment, Shaanxi took concrete measures in ensuring the virtuous circle and healthy development of the real estate industry. By focusing on the housing problems, Shaanxi worked out practical solutions to the housing problems of urban poor people.

Altogether 22.964 billion yuan was invested in the low-income housing projects of the whole province, and 10,239 new houses and apartments were put into construction in the shanty town renovation projects, with 29,815 basically completed. Urban housing security family rental subsidies were granted to 42,678 households, with 5,068 new public renting houses and 22,421 new low-income rental houses put into construction respectively. A total of 3,634 urban old communities were put into reconstruction, benefiting 393,400 families.

咸阳市淳化县十里塬镇易地扶贫搬迁集中安置点

4. 就业 Employment

2021 年是陕西省巩固拓展脱贫攻坚成果同乡村振兴有效衔接的起步之年。陕西坚持把稳岗就业作为巩固拓展脱贫攻坚成果同乡村振兴有效衔接的重点工作，紧盯“脱贫不稳定户、边缘易致贫户和突发严重困难户”三类人员，突出“乡村振兴重点帮扶县、脱贫群众、搬迁群众”三个重点，聚焦“稳输出、拓渠道、提能力、优服务”

The year 2021 marks the beginning for Shaanxi Province to consolidate and expand the achievements of poverty alleviation and then link them with the efforts of rural revitalization. To achieve such effective connection, Shaanxi gives top priority to stabilizing employment and pays close attention to three key groups, including those who have just emerged from poverty but whose position is far from secure, those on the verge of poverty who can fall back in again easily, and those experiencing difficulties in meeting their basic needs due to expenditure induced by illness. It also gives prominence to three key issues of "key counties for receiving assistance for rural revitalization, the poor who have been lifted out of poverty and resettled population" while focusing on "stabilizing output, expanding

金银花特色产业助力乡村振兴

咸阳市永寿县绿菜公司开发岗位吸纳贫困户就业

四个关键。2021 年，全省脱贫群众外出务工人数累计达到 216.43 万人，是上年的 102.9%，较上年增加 6.2 万人。

channels, improving capabilities, and optimizing services". A total of 2.1643 million people in the province, who had been lifted out of poverty, worked away from their hometown in 2021, an increase of 102.9% (62,000) compared with the previous year.

老少同乐

5. 社会保障 Social Security

2021 年，陕西建成各类养老机构及服务设施 1.65 万个，有各类养老床位 27.6 万张，城市社区日间照料中心、农村互助幸福院覆盖率分别达到

In 2021, 16,500 elderly care institutions and service facilities, and 276,000 various aged care beds were offered in Shaanxi. The coverage rates of urban community daycare centers and rural mutual aid and happiness homes for the

便民医保办理

57.2%、83%；建成 100 个救助管理机构、86 个殡仪馆、183 座公墓、48 个民政福利园区，覆盖 44% 的县（区）。

elderly reached 57.2% and 83% respectively. Shaanxi has also established 100 assistance institutions, 86 funeral homes, 183 cemeteries, and 48 civil affairs welfare parks, covering 44% of the counties (districts).

6. 公共文化服务 Public Cultural Service

2021 年中国秦腔优秀剧目会演惠及线上线下观众 600 余万人次，第七届丝绸之路国际艺术节吸引观众 1300 余万人次。

陕西建成文化馆分馆 948 个、图书馆分馆 1036 个、城市书房等新型公共文化空间 444 个。推出惠民举措 130 余项，发放惠民卡券 70 余万张。陕西“戏曲进乡村”演出 1.34 万场次。建成陕

In 2021, the excellent performances of Chinese Qin Opera have benefited more than 6 million audiences. The 7th Silk Road International Arts Festival has attracted over 13 million viewers.

In Shaanxi, 948 branches of cultural centers, 1,036 branches of libraries, and 444 new public cultural spaces such as urban study rooms have been established. More than 130 measures to benefit the public were launched, and more than 700,000 coupons were issued by the local authorities. The program "Sending Operas to the Countryside" has given 13,400 performances. 6 demonstration application scenarios of "5G + culture

第七届丝绸之路国际电影节开幕式

农家书屋

艺术下乡丰富群众文化生活

西“5G+ 文旅”示范应用场景 6 个、智慧旅游项目 2 个。乡村旅游惠及农户 34.45 万户 124.01 万人，带动农村就业 69.37 万人，同比增长 9.28%、9.17% 和 9.27%。

tourism" and 2 smart tourism projects have been completed. Rural tourism has benefited 344,500 rural households, including 1,240,100 people, and created 693,700 jobs in rural areas, a year-on-year increase of 9.28%, 9.17%, and 9.27% respectively.

形式多样的公共文化服务

乡村振兴 Rural Revitalization

2021 年是陕西“三农”工作重心发生历史性变化的一年，全省 56 个贫困县全部摘帽，465 万建档立卡贫困人口全部脱贫，绝对贫困和区域性整体贫困问题得到历史性解决。

在省委、省政府的坚强领导下，全省上下敬终如始，顽强拼搏，逐一破解体制转型、任务转

安康市石泉县中池镇现代农业产业园区

2021 witnessed the historic shifts in the focus of Shaanxi's work related to agriculture, rural areas and farmers. With 56 impoverished counties and 4.65 million registered households living under the poverty line over the province being lifted out of poverty, the problems of absolute poverty and regional poverty have been historically resolved.

Under the strong leadership of the Provincial Party Committee and the Provincial Government, the whole province has worked hard to solve the difficulties of system transformation, task change and work transition one after another, and established and improved the "five mechanisms", thus establishing the system of "multiple pillars" with efficient connection of all fields. Shaanxi made consolidating and building

变、工作转轨的难题，建立健全“五项机制”，创造性地立起了有效衔接的四梁八柱。把巩固拓展脱贫攻坚成果作为首要任务，聚焦“两不愁三保障”和饮水安全，深入开展到村“六查”、入户“六问”和电话随机抽查等活动，切实守住了不发生规模性返贫的底线。以灾情疫情为令，果断应对，全力消除灾情疫情影响。大力推动脱贫地区特色产业提质增效、扎实做好稳岗就业、突出支持重点帮扶县发展、全力推进易地搬迁后续扶持等工作。在国家乡村振兴局2021年的11项重点工作中，我省有8项工作在全国经验交流会上交流经验或在我省召开现场会推广。

on achievements in poverty alleviation a top priority, focusing on ensuring poor people do not have to worry about food and clothing and have access to compulsory education, basic medical services and safe housing, as well as the safety of drinking water. Intensive activities such as "six checks" in villages, "six inquiries" in households, and random telephone inspections were carried out, so as to ensure no large-scale return to poverty. We responded resolutely to disasters and Covid-19, striving to eliminate their impacts. We vigorously promoted the quality and efficiency improvement of specialty industries in poverty alleviation areas, took solid measures in stabilizing employment, gave prominent support to the development of key counties receiving assistance, and spared no effort in promoting the follow-up support for people who were relocated from inhospitable areas. Among the 11 key tasks listed by the National Rural Development Administration, we have exchanged our experience at eight of them at the national meeting, or held on-site promotion in Shaanxi Province.

杨凌智慧农业示范园区

汉中油菜花海

高西沟村
——黄土高原的治理典范

Gaoxigou Village:
A Model of Good Governesson the Loess Plateau

米脂县高西沟村位于陕北黄土高原丘陵沟壑区，总面积 4 平方千米。曾经的高西沟村荒芜贫瘠，水土流失严重。“山上光秃秃，下面黄水流，年年遭灾害，十年九不收。”这段顺口溜描述了60 多年前高西沟的自然生态情况。

20 世纪 70 年代，经过初期的实践，高西沟人逐步确立了“宜粮则粮、宜林则林、宜牧则牧”的原则，形成了用三分之一的土地植树造林、用三分之一的土地种草养牧、用三分之一的土地种粮务农的“三三制”模式，使高西沟村在解决了

Gaoxigou Village is located in Mizhi County in northern Shaanxi, with a total area of four square kilometers. Sitting in the hilly gullied area of the Loess Plateau, the village was once bleak and barren due to serious soil erosion. Bare hillside, under which turbid water follows, Disasters year and year leave no grain to farmers.The doggerel vividly depicts the ecological environment of Gaoxigou Village more than six decades ago.

In the 1970s, after the initial trial, villagers of Gaoxigou gradually established the principle of "planting crops, trees or grass based on conditions", and formed a "three-thirds system", with the land for trees and forests, the land for grass and pasture, and the land to grow crops for agriculture accounting for one third of the total land area respectively. This system guaranteed the food supply in Gaoxigou and significantly improved

高西沟新貌

村民吃饭问题的同时，生态环境也得到了极大改善，实现了“泥不下山，洪水不出沟，不向黄河输送泥沙”。

进入 21 世纪后，高西沟人又积极响应时代的号召，走上生态与经济协调发展、人与自然和谐共存的良性循环路子，形成了林、牧、农“三二一”的新生态产业结构，即三份林地、二份草地、一份田地。

作为水土保持生态建设的先行者，如今的高西沟“梯田层层盘山头，金秋果香飘满沟”。有生态林 2300 亩、经济林 1000 亩、大小淤地坝 126 座，林草覆盖率达 70%。树林、果园和牧草，把黄土山装扮得郁郁葱葱。

高西沟村还以绿色财富为依托，发展生态旅游，吸引越来越多的游客在黄土褶皱中享受“江南好风景”。青山绿水中，小米和苹果种植、养羊等产业也红火了起来。村民们曾经望穿了眼的美好日子就在当下。

the local environment, keeping silt within mountains instead of flowing into the Yellow River.

Entering the 21st century, villagers of Gaoxigou have actively followed the trend of the times, got on the circular track of sound development characterized by coordinated ecological and economic development and harmonious coexistence of man and nature, and formed a new ecological industrial structure of forestry, animal husbandry and agriculture, with forest land, grassland and farmland developing in the proportion of 3:2:1.

Nowadays in Gaoxigou, the Loess Plateau is lushly dressed by woods, orchards and pasture. The village now enjoys a forest and grass coverage rate of 70%, with 2,300 mu of ecological forestry, 1,000 mu of economic forestry, 126 large and small silt dams.

Based on its green wealth, Gaoxigou village vigorously develops ecological tourism, attracting a growing number of tourists to enjoy the "wonderful southern scenery" in the folds of loess. What was out of reach is now a reality. Gaoxigou, a forerunner in soil conservation and ecological development, now features layers of terraces atop mountains and fruit trees with strong aroma spreading everywhere in the valley. Amidst the lush mountains and lucid waters, industries such as millet and apple planting and sheep raising are flourishing.

陕西是“一带一路”建设的重要节点。陕西已与近 200 个国家和地区建立了经贸联系。世界 500 强企业在陕西投资企业 144 家。中国（陕西）自由贸易试验区正在加快建设，在陕西举办的重大经贸和外事活动越来越多，陕西正在以更加自信的姿态走向世界。

Shaanxi holds great importance in "the Belt and the Road Initiative" and has made business connections with about 200 countries and regions. 144 of the world's top 500 enterprises have made investment in Shaanxi. The construction of China (Shaanxi) Pilot Free Trade Zone is speeding up, and more and more important trade and foreign affairs activities are held in Shaanxi. Shaanxi is embracing the world with growing confidence.

Chapter Five

第五篇

海纳百川，兼容并包

百川衮衮东赴海

Embracing and All-inclusive

All Rivers Flowing East to the Sea

融入『一带一路』

Response to "the Belt and Road Initiative"

2021 年，陕西全省上下贯通落实习近平总书记来陕考察重要讲话精神，积极应对外部环境的深刻变化，统筹推进新冠肺炎疫情防控和“一带一路”建设高质量发展，围绕打造内陆改革开放高地目标，加快构筑开放大通道、大平台，有力有序推进“一带一路”五大中心建设，相关领域呈现诸多亮点。

In 2021, Shaanxi has thoroughly implemented the spirit of General Secretary Xi Jinping's important speech during his inspection of Shaanxi and created highlights in several fields. It has actively responded to the profound changes in its external environment, coordinated Covid-19 control and the high-quality development of the Belt and Road Initiative. Focusing on building an inland highland for reform and opening up, Shaanxi has sped up the construction of major transit routes and major platforms for opening up, and promoted the construction of five major centers of the Belt and Road Initiative in a vigorous and orderly manner.

“一带一路”农业合作部（州）长圆桌会议

1. 中欧班列（西安）累计开行过万列
The China-Europe Railway Express Amounting to over 10,000 Trips

中欧班列（西安）年度开行 3841 列，运送货物 287.3 万吨，历年累计开行 11415 列，核心指标稳居全国前列。开通日韩过境货物测试班列，常态化开行跨境电商专列，国际干线增加至 16 条，“+ 西欧”集结线路达 15 条。推进港区一体化，设立西安国际港站，整体装卸能力提升 30%。上线运营中欧班列“长安号”数字金融综合服务平台，启动“铁路进出境快速通关业务”，通关时间压缩 1/2。

The China-Europe Railway Express (Xi'an) marked 3,841 trips in 2021, transporting 2.873 million tons of goods. The total number of trips has reached 11,415, and the core indicators held the leading position in the country. China Railway Express has conducted the first trial run for Japan-South Korea transit cargo train services, and a special train for cross-border e-commerce was operated on a regular basis. The number of international trunk lines added up to 16, and the number of "+ Western Europe" assembly lines reached 15. Shaanxi has worked hard to promote the integration of port areas, and set up Xi'an International Port Station, with the overall loading and unloading capacity rising by 30%. The Digital Financial Service Platform of China Railway "Express Chang'an" was launched with the new business model of "Railway Inbound and Outbound Rapid Customs Clearance". The overall customs clearance time was shortened by 50%.

2. 空中丝绸之路建设全面提速
Speeding up the Construction the Silk Road in the Air

新开通莫斯科—西安—阿拉木图第五航权货运航线，第五航权货运航线累计达 3 条。西北国际货航正式首航，全货运航线累计达 38 条，完成货邮吞吐量 39.56 万吨，位列全国机场第九位。承接国际分流航班 243 架次，入境旅客 2.86 万人次。空港型国家物流枢纽成功获批，临空经济产值突破 120 亿元。

The Moscow–Xi'an–Almaty 5th–freedom cargo route was launched, amounting to 3 routes. Northwest International Cargo was officially put into operation with 38 all–cargo routes, and the cargo and mail throughput totaled 395,600 tons, ranking 9th among China's airports. It has accommodated 243 international diverted flights and 28,600 inbound passengers. The Shaanxi Airport–type National Logistics Hub has been approved, and the airport economic output exceeded 12 billion yuan.

空中丝绸之路建设全面提速

杨凌小麦新品种在哈萨克斯坦“中哈”现代农业创新示范园再次获得丰收

3. 上合组织农业技术交流培训示范基地实质性运行 SCO Agricultural Technology Exchange and Training Demonstration Base Officially Opened

上合农业基地建设《构想》通过第六届上合组织成员国农业部长会审议，成为首个上合组织成员国“共商、共建、共享”的农业交流合作平台，并被上合组织成员国杜尚别峰会列入 20 年农业合作重要成果。哈萨克斯坦和乌兹别克斯坦 2 家境外农业技术实训基地揭牌，上合组织成员国涉农高校联盟成立，上合组织现代农业交流中心启用，组织面向上合组织国家援外培训 8 期，举办“云讲座”9 期。

The "Proposal" for establishing the SCO Agricultural Technology Exchange and Training Demonstration Base was reviewed and approved by the 6th Meeting of the Agriculture Ministers of SCO member states. The demonstration base has become the first agricultural exchange and cooperation platform among SCO member states with the principle of "Wide Consultation, Joint Contribution and Shared Benefits", which was listed by the Dushanbe Summit as one of the important achievements of agricultural cooperation in the past 20 years. 2 overseas agricultural technology training bases in Kazakhstan and Uzbekistan were officially launched, and the agriculture-related university alliance in SCO member states was established. It has also launched the SCO Modern Agriculture Exchange Center, by which 8 sessions of the foreign-aid training program for SCO member states were organized and 9 online lectures were held.

4. 成功承办“中国＋中亚五国”外长第二次会晤

Successful Hosting the 2nd "China + Central Asia" (C + C5) Foreign Ministers' Meeting

“中国＋中亚五国”外长第二次会晤在西安举行，此次会晤是疫情发生以来中方首次主办的多边外长会议。会晤达成多项共识和成果，丝绸之路考古合作研究中心、中国—中亚农业合作中心、传统医学中心、减贫惠农计划、教育培训计划和综合农业科技示范园区等6项涉陕成果加速落地。西北大学“中国—中亚人类与环境‘一带一路’联合实验室”获批国家第三批“一带一路”联合实验室。

The 2nd "China + Central Asia" (C+C5) Foreign Ministers' Meeting was held in Xi'an, which was also the first multilateral foreign ministers' meeting hosted by China since the outbreak of the pandemic. The meeting has reached a wide range of consensuses and achievements concerning 6 Shaanxi-related issues such as the establishment of Silk Road Archaeology Cooperation Research Center, the China-Central Asia Agricultural Cooperation Center, the Traditional Medicine Center, the Poverty Alleviation and Farming Program, the Education and Training Program, and the Comprehensive Agricultural Science and Technology Demonstration Park. "The Belt and Road Joint Laboratory on China-Central Asia Human and Environment" of Northwest University was approved as the third batch of national Belt and Road joint laboratories.

“国风秦韵——陕西文创上合国家巡展”在巴基斯坦受热捧

第五届丝绸之路国际博览会暨中国东西部合作与投资贸易洽谈会开幕式

5. “一带一路”国际规则标准“软联通”积极推进 Active Promotion of the Soft Connectivity of the Belt and Road International Rules and Standards

“一带一路”国家计量测试研究中心（陕西）在西安揭牌，成为全国首家服务“一带一路”倡议的国家级计量技术研究机构。成功举办了“一带一路”国际交通研讨会，启动了《共建“一带一路”国家汽车行业碳排放标准》研究项目。对接国际贸易规则，西安市入选第三轮中欧区域政策合作中方案例地区。

The Belt and Road National Metrology and Testing Research Center (Shaanxi) was officially launched in Xi'an, becoming the first national metrology research institution to serve the Belt and Road Initiative. It also held the Belt and Road International Transport Symposium, during which the research project "Co-constructing the Belt and Road National Automobile Industry Carbon Emission Standard" was launched. In line with international trade rules, Xi'an was listed as the Chinese case area for the 3rd round of China-EU regional policy cooperation.

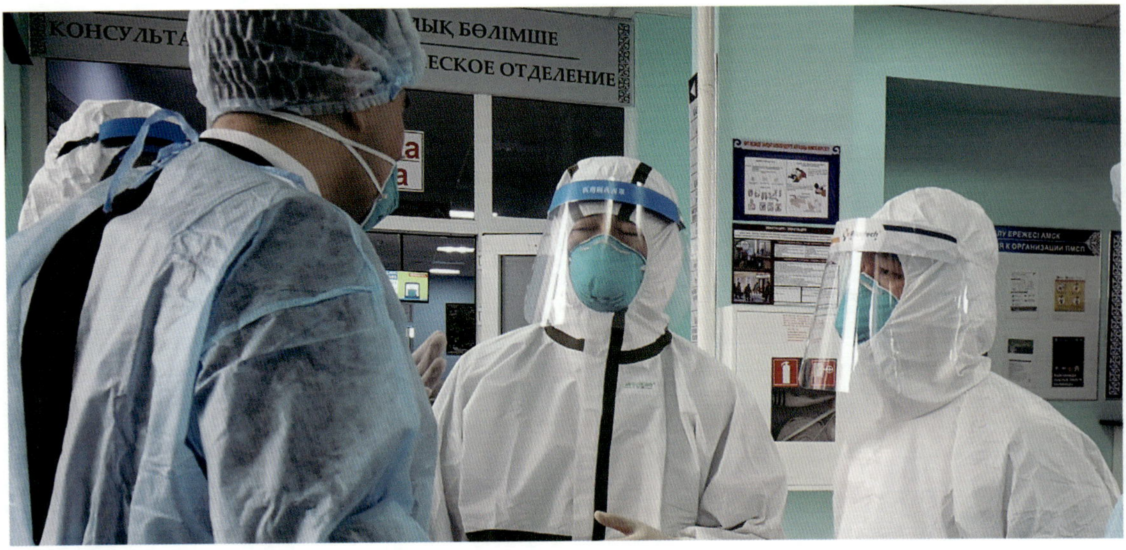

援外医疗队与当地医生交流经验

6. 中国（陕西）赴塔吉克斯坦医疗卫生联合工作组被授予国际友谊贡献奖

China (Shaanxi) Joint Working Group to Tajikistan Conferred International Contribution Award

积极开展国际医疗卫生援助，由我省派遣的中国（陕西）赴塔吉克斯坦医疗卫生联合工作组圆满完成抗疫合作任务，受到塔政府和中国外交部广泛好评，被授予国际友谊贡献奖。2021 年是我省援外医疗队派遣 50 周年，累计向苏丹、马拉维、瓦努阿图派遣援外医疗队 50 批，诊治患者 836.8 万人次。

Shaanxi took the initiative in conducting international medical and healthcare assistance. China (Shaanxi) Joint Working Group to Tajikistan from Shaanxi successfully finished the cooperation task against Covid-19, which won widespread praise from the Tajikistan government and Ministry of Foreign Affairs of China, and was conferred International Friendship Contribution Award. 2021 marked the 50th anniversary of Shaanxi's medical teams sent abroad, adding up to 50 times of sending medical teams to Sudan, Malawi, and Vanuatu, treating 8.368 million patients.

7. “通丝路”平台成功接入人民币跨境支付系统

Successful Integration of RMB SilkRoad Platform into CIPS

开放领域金融服务体系加快完善，“通丝路”跨境电商人民币结算服务平台成功接入CIPS（人民币跨境支付系统）标准收发器，成为西北地区首家部署CIPS标准收

The financial service system in the open sectors was further perfected. RMB SilkRoad Cross Border E-commerce RMB Settlement Service Platform was successfully integrated into CIPS Standard Transceiver, making it the first e-commerce platform to do so in Northwestern China. Innovative

发器的电商平台。创新推出“中欧班列贷”、自贸港商票“运单融资”等产品，设立跨境人民币优质企业“白名单”。推动贸易外汇收支便利化试点增量扩面，截至12月底，省内4家银行、11家企业加入试点，办理金额59.44亿美元。

products such as "China-Europe Railway Express Loan" and "Waybill Financing" of Free Trade Port Commercial Tickets were launched, and a "white list" of cross-border RMB high-quality enterprises was established. With the efforts exerted in increasing the number and coverage of trade and foreign exchange revenue and expenditure trials, 4 banks and 11 enterprises in Shaanxi Province have joined the trial by the end of last December, with a processing amount of US $5.944 billion.

8. 对外经贸合作持续推进高质量发展

Foreign Economic and Trade Cooperation Continuing Promoting High-quality Development

成功举办2021“丝路电商”合作（西安）圆桌会。邀请奥地利等20个国家和地区驻华使领馆及官方机构代表，围绕跨境电商领域有效利用中欧班列长安号物流通道，开展跨境电商产业多边国际合作和人才培训等共同研讨，并向各国发布《中欧班列长安号跨境电商全国集结中心发展三年行动计划》。对“一带一路”沿线国家（地区）进出口同比增长28.2%，投资同比增长26.4%。

The 2021 The Silk Road E-commerce Cooperation Roundtable Conference (Xi'an) was successfully held. Representatives of embassies, consulates and official institutions in China from Austria and other 20 countries and regions were invited to attend the conference focusing on topics of effective use of the logistics channel of the China-Europe Railway "Express Chang'an" in the field of cross-border e-commerce, and multilateral international cooperation and talent training in this field. During the conference, The Three-year Development Action Plan of the China-Europe Railway Express Chang 'an Cross-border E-commerce Assembly Center was issued. The total export and import volume to countries and regions of the Belt and Road Initiative increased by 28.2% and the investment increased by 26.4% on a year-on-year base.

完善开放领域金融服务体系，推动跨境贸易项目合作

自贸区建设
Free Zone Construction

陕西自贸试验区自2017年4月揭牌运行以来，围绕战略定位和发展目标深入开展制度创新，有效融入和服务国家重大战略，对全省深

Since its launch in April 2017, Shaanxi Pilot Free Trade Zone has carried out in-depth institutional innovation by centering on its strategic positioning and development goals. Effectively integrating and serving major national strategies, it has played a leading and exemplary role

中国（陕西）自由贸易试验区

化改革、扩大开放发挥了引领示范作用。

2021 年陕西持续深化自贸试验区改革创新，全年陕西自贸试验区新增市场主体 3.34 万家，同比增长 102.7%，新增企业 17825 家，同比增长 29.2%。

in deepening reform and opening wider to the outside world in Shaanxi Province.

In 2021, Shaanxi continued to deepen reform and innovation in the Pilot Free Trade Zone, with an increase of 33,400 new market entities, a year-on-year increase of 102.7%, and an increase of 17,825 new enterprises, a year-on-year increase of 29.2%.

1. 保障机制不断完善
Guarantee Mechanism Keeping Perfecting

2021年陕西省颁布《中国（陕西）自由贸易试验区条例》，出台《中国（陕西）自由贸易试验区进一步深化改革开放实施方案》，加快将自贸试验区建设成全面改革开放试验田、内陆改革开放高地、“一带一路”经济合作和人文交流重要支点，自贸试验区“证照分离”改革全面实施。制度创新成果丰硕，成立9个自贸工作专题组，确定第一批34项重点改革创新事项，探索形成6项首创性改革创新经验，总结形成94个改革创新案例，其中8项创新成果在全国复制推广、30项在全省复制推广，为全省开放型经济发展注入新动力。

In 2021, Shaanxi issued China (Shaanxi) Pilot Free Trade Zone Regulations, and introduced Implementation Plan for Deepening Reform and Opening Wider to the Outside World in China (Shaanxi) Pilot Free Trade Zone, accelerating the progress of making the free trade area a pilot ground for all-round reform and opening-up, an inland highland of reform and opening-up, and an important base for the Belt and Road economic cooperation and cultural exchange. The reform of separating operating permits and business licenses was fully implemented in the Pilot Free Trade Zone. We have made fruitful achievements in system innovation. 9 free trade work groups were set up, and the first batch of 34 key items of reform and innovation were identified. We gained 6 initiative innovation experience, and formed 94 reform and innovation cases. Among them, 8 were copied and promoted nationwide, 30 were recommended over the province, injecting new momentum for the development of open economy in Shaanxi.

自贸试验区改革全面实施

中俄丝路创新园

2. 特色产业加快聚集
Assembling of Specialty Industries Taking up Speed

2021 年西北地区最大的微生物测序中心等入驻陕西自贸试验区，临空产业、跨境电商、医疗康养、数字文创等新业态新模式不断涌现。协同发展稳步推进，陕西省推动自贸试验区与秦创原创新驱动平台相互赋能。筹建黄河流域自贸试验区联盟，实现西安区域与济南、兰州等 13 个城市政务服务事项“跨省通办”。“一带一路”国际商事法律服务示范区建设扎实推进。

In 2021, the largest microbial sequencing center in Northwestern China was set up in Shaanxi Pilot Free Trade Zone, and new industrial patterns such as airport industry, cross-border e-commerce, medical and health care industry, and digital cultural and creative industry have been springing up. The coordinated development in Shaanxi has been promoted steadily. The mutual empowerment of Shaanxi Pilot Free Trade Zone and the Qinchuangyuan Innovation-driven General Platform was promoted, and the alliance of the pilot free trade zones in the Yellow River Basin was planned to establish, realizing the "Inter-Provincial Government Services" between Xi'an and 13 cities, including Jinan and Lanzhou. The establishment of the Belt and Road Demonstration Zone for International Commercial Legal Services (BRD-ICLS) was undergoing with solid progress.

“汉风——中国汉代文物展”在法国举行

国际交流合作

International Exchange and Cooperation

1. 全省国际友好城市数量超百对

Shaanxi Boasting over 100 International Sister Cities

2021年，陕西不断扩大国际“朋友圈”，全省国际友好城市总数达101对，省级友好城市28对，市级友好城市73对，遍布五大洲41个国家，实现中亚地区全覆盖。以“项目友好城市”为抓手，整合经贸旅游、文化艺术等优势，成功举办了“面向未来——朱鹮发现40年中日韩线上纪念活动”“新时代斯诺”国际论坛等活动。

Shaanxi has continued to expand its international "friend circle" and established sister-city relations with 101 cities in 41 countries of five continents, including 28 at provincial level and 73 at city level, achieving full coverage in Central Asia. Focusing on "Establishing Sister-City Friendship by Projects", Shaanxi has conducted various activities such as "Facing the Future — China-Japan-South Korea Online Commemoration Activity for the 40th Anniversary of the Rediscovery of the Crested Ibis" and the "Legacy of the Snows in New Era" International Forum, with the integration of the resources in economy, trade, tourism, culture and art.

“秦始皇和兵马俑展” 在英国利物浦国家博物馆举行

2. 国际贸易新业态新模式加快发展

New Business Form and Mode in International Trade Speeding Up Development

西安市中医药服务“走出去”新模式、金融助推贸易转型升级新模式等 5 个案例入选国家全面深化服务贸易创新发展试点“最佳实践案例”。西安市获批国家加工贸易产业园，曲江新区列为第二批国家文化出口基地。西安跨境电商综合试验区建设成效凸显，跨境电商交易额增长 46.3%，累计建设运营海外仓 80 余个。

5 cases of Shaanxi were selected as "Best Practice Cases" in the National Comprehensive Deepening Trade Services Innovative Development Trial Programs, including the new models of Traditional Chinese Medicine Services "Going Global" and Boosting Trade Transformation and Upgrading through Finance. Xi'an was approved to establish the National Processing Trade Industrial Park, and Qujiang New District was listed in the second batch of national cultural export bases. The construction of Xi'an Cross-border E-commerce Comprehensive Pilot Zone has achieved outstanding results, with the transaction volume growth of 46.3%, amounting to more than 80 overseas warehouses.

第五届丝绸之路国际博览会上展出的厨余垃圾处理设备

第 28 届杨凌农高会上展出的污水循环利用智能化节水灌溉模型

3. 丝博会、农高会、欧亚经济论坛创新举办 The Silk Expo, CAF and the Euro-Asia Economic Forum Successfully Held

丝博会、农高会、欧亚经济论坛采取线上线下相结合模式成功举办。丝博会展览展示面积、参展企业、展品种类创历史新高；农高会集中展示了 9000 多项最新农业科技成果及先进适用技术；欧亚经济论坛创新一会一展模式，首次同期举办中国（陕西）进出口商品展，现场意向交易金额达 25.46 亿元。投资贸易促进功能持续提升，全省实际利用外资增长 21.4%，引进内资增长 23.8%。

The Silk Expo, the China Yangling Agricultural Hi-Tech Fair (CAF) and the Euro-Asia Economic Forum were held in the offline and online blended mode. The exhibition area, number of exhibitors, and types of exhibits in the Silk Expo reached a record high. More than 9,000 latest agricultural scientific and technological achievements and advanced and applicable technologies were displayed at the China Yangling Agricultural Hi-Tech Fair (CAF). The Euro-Asia Economic Forum created a one-meeting-one-exhibition model and held the China (Shaanxi) Import and Export Commodities Exhibition for the first time, with an on-site transaction volume of 2.546 billion yuan. The promotion function of investment and trade is improving steadily, with a 21.4% increase of actual utilization of foreign capital and 23.8% increase of receiving domestic capital across the province.

2022年陕西经济社会发展主要目标

Major Social and Economic Goals of Shaanxi Province in 2022

生产总值增长 6% 左右，一般公共预算收入增长 3% 左右，城乡居民收入分别增长 6.5% 和 8% 左右。引进内资、实际利用外资分别增长 12%、15% 以上。社会消费品零售总额增长 7.5% 左右。城镇新增就业 40 万人以上，城镇调查失业率 5.5% 以内，居民消费价格涨幅 3% 左右，粮食产量 240 亿斤以上。能耗强度在“十四五”规划期内统筹考核。

In 2022, GDP of Shaanxi is expected to grow by 6%, with a 3% increase in the general public budget revenue, 6.5% and 8% increase in the income of urban and rural residents respectively, over 12% and 15% increase in the introduction of domestic capital and the actual utilization of foreign capital respectively, and 7.5% increase in total retail sales of social consumer goods. Over 400,000 new jobs will be created in urban areas, and the surveyed unemployment rate will be controlled under 5.5% in urban areas. The consumer prices will rise by about 3%, and the grain yield will exceed 12 billion kg. The energy consumption intensity will be comprehensively assessed during the 14th Five-Year Plan period.

隆基绿能太阳能光伏电站

"长安号"中欧班列

China-Europe Railway Express "Chang'an Express"

中欧班列"长安号"是中国西安始发的国际货运班列，是陕西省和西安市促进外向型经济建设的重要抓手。在各方有力推动下，中欧班列"长安号"已发展成为全国线路最全、覆盖最广、效率最高、速度最快的国际货运班列，为陕西更好融入共建"一带一路"大格局注入强劲动力。

2021 年 8 月 11 日，一列满载布料、载客电梯、暖气片等货物的 X9041 次中欧班列（西安），从西安国际港站开出，驶向哈萨克斯坦阿拉木图。这是陕西累计开行的第 10000 列中欧班列。

从 2013 年第 1 列"长安号"开行，到 2020 年全年累计开行 3720 列，再到如今累计开行突破 10000 列，"长安号"奔跑速度不断加快，运输的货物品类也由最初的钻井设备增加至纺织制品、橡胶制品、电子产品、汽车整车及配件等 9 大类，开行

China-Europe Railway Express "Chang'an Express", an international freight train departing from Xi'an, China, is the crux for Xi'an City and Shaanxi Province to promote the development of export-oriented economy. With the strong support of all parties, "Chang'an Express" has developed into China's fastest international freight train with the most lines, the widest coverage and the highest efficiency, injecting strong momentum for Shaanxi to better integrate into "the Belt and Road" Initiative.

On August 11, 2021, an X9041 China-Europe Railway Express (Xi'an) departed from Xi'an International Port Station and headed for Almaty, Kazakhstan, loaded with fabrics, passenger elevators, heaters and other goods. This marks the 10,000th cumulative railway express trips from Shaanxi.

Since 2013 when the first "Chang'an Express" was lunched, the train is going at a higher speed, with 3,720 trips made in 2020 and the total trips exceeding 10,000 this year. The cargo transported by "Chang'an Express" has expanded from drilling equipment at the start to goods of 9 major categories such as textile products, rubber products, electronic products, automobile vehicles and accessories, etc. The railway express now travels along 15 international routes and has reached 44 countries and regions, basically

中欧班列“长安号”

的国际线路增加至 15 条，覆盖 44 个国家和地区，基本实现中亚、南亚、西亚及欧洲地区主要货源地全覆盖。“长安号”的始发站——西安国际港站也从一个只有 7 条线路的四等小站，发展成拥有 17 条到发线、6 条调车线、19 条货物线、4 条集装箱中心站配置装卸线和 15 台门吊的一等站，集装箱年吞吐量最高可达 90 万标箱，运输能力比 2013 年提升了 280.37%。

8 年间，“长安号”的辐射作用也由“线”及“面”加速拓展。依托欧亚地区全覆盖的国际货运网络和“西欧”集结体系，“长安号”吸引国内 29 个省的货物在西安港集散分拨，辐射长三角、珠三角、京津冀等主要货源地。目前，长安号运输的省外货物占比超过 75%，进口货物中 65% 以上从西安分拨至全国，西安已成为辐射全国、连通欧亚的货物集散中转枢纽。

covering all main cargo producers in Central Asia, South Asia, West Asia and Europe. Xi'an International Port Station, the departure station of "Chang'an Express", has also developed from a small fourth-class station with mere 7 lines to a first-class station with 17 arrival and departure lines, 6 shunting lines, 19 cargo lines, 4 loading and unloading lines of container central station and 15 gantry cranes. The annual container throughput can reach up to 900,000 TEUs of containers, an increase of 280.37% in the transportation capacity from 2013.

During the past 8 years, "Chang'an Express" has stimulated the development of related areas. With its full-coverage international freight network in Eurasia and the consolidation system in Western Europe, "Chang'an Express" has attracted 29 provinces to collect and distribute goods in Xi'an, radiating the Yangtze River Delta, Pearl River Delta, Beijing-Tianjin-Hebei region and other major cargo sources in China. At present, more than 75% of the cargoes transported by Chang'an Express are from other provinces and over 65% of the imported cargoes are distributed from Xi'an to corners in China. Xi'an has become a cargo distribution and transit hub that radiates the whole country and connects Europe and Asia.

关山晨牧

Annex

附录

›

附录一
三秦城市概览

Annex I
Overview of Major Cities in Shaanxi Province

千年古都，常来长安

Xi'an, a city of thousands of years of history, is welcoming friends near and afar

西安古称长安，是陕西省省会，世界历史文化名城，国家重要的科研、教育和工业基地。作为古丝绸之路的起点，西安正在向亚欧合作交流的国际化大都市迈进。

Xi'an, known as Chang'an in ancient times, is the capital of Shaanxi, a famous historical and cultural city in the world, an important base for science, education and industries of China. As the starting point of ancient Silk Road, Xi'an is developing to be an international metropolis for Eurasian cooperation and exchanges.

青铜之乡　文明宝鸡

Baoji, hometown of bronze ware with brilliant civilization

宝鸡古称陈仓，是陕西省第二大城市，也是我国承接东西、连通南北的重要交通枢纽。宝鸡是我国西部工业重镇，有“中国钛谷”之称。

Baoji, known as Chencang in ancient times, is the second largest city of Shaanxi and an important traffic hub linking the east with the west, and the north with the south. Baoji is also an important industrial city in western China. It is also known as the "Titanium Valley of China".

大秦故都　德善咸阳

Xianyang, capital of the Qin Dynasty and land of virtue

咸阳是中华民族繁荣富强的发端地和秦文化的发源地，也是中国大地原点所在地、中国农耕文明的发祥地。咸阳现已发展成为国家重要的商品粮生产基地和优质苹果、蔬菜生产基地。

Xianyang is the cradle of prosperous and powerful China and a source of the Qin civilization. It is the geodetic origin of China. It has a sound agricultural basis and is the birthplace of China's farming civilization. Today, Xianyang is an important base for commodity grain, high-quality apples and vegetables in China.

药王故里　五彩铜川

Tongchuan, beautiful hometown of Herb King

铜川是药王孙思邈故里，也是中国红色革命的根据地、黑色煤炭的富集地和绿色生态的养生地。耀州窑久负盛名，中国历史文化名镇陈炉被誉为“东方古陶瓷生产活化石”。

Tongchuan is the home town of Herb King Sun Simiao. It is also a revolutionary base, a place with plentiful coal and an ecological land for regimen. Yaozhou Kiln has enjoyed a high reputation for a long time. Chenlu, a famous Chinese historical and cultural town, is honored as a "living fossil for oriental ancient ceramics production".

三圣故里 人文渭南

Weinan, the Home of Three Saints with humanity

渭南是中华民族的重要发祥地，是中国的戏曲之乡和民俗之乡。渭南工农业齐头并进，既被称为陕西的“粮仓”“棉库”，也有“中国钼都”“华夏金城”之誉。

Weinan is an important cradle of the Chinese nation and also known as a hometown for operas and folk customs. Both industry and agriculture are well-developed in Weinan. As the "Granary" and "Cotton Warehouse" of Shaanxi, Weinan also has the titles of "capital of molybdenum" and "gold city" of China for its plentiful mineral resources.

革命圣地 魅力延安

Yan'an, a charming and holy revolutionary land

延安是历史文化名城，全国优秀旅游城市和爱国主义、革命传统、延安精神三大教育基地。延安旅游资源独具特色，旅游业具有广阔前景；矿产资源丰富，是中国石油工业的发祥地。

Yan'an is one of famous historical and cultural cities, national excellent tourism cities, and an education base for patriotism, revolutionary tradition and the Yan'an spirit. Yan'an has unique cultural tourism resources and great potential in tourism. Yan'an boasts abundant mineral resources. It is the cradle land of China's petroleum industry.

能源新都 幸福榆林

Yulin, new capital of energy and great place for a happy life

榆林素有“九边重镇”之美誉，是国家历史文化名城。榆林自古多元文化交汇，集边塞、游牧、黄土、红色文化于一体。榆林能源富集，是建设中的国家能源化工基地。

Yulin has been known as a "key frontier city". As one of famous historical and cultural cities, Yulin has been a hub of diverse cultures, such as frontier culture, nomadic culture, loess culture and revolutionry culture, since ancient times. Boasting rich mineral resources, Yulin is a national energy and chemical base under construction.

两汉三国 真美汉中

Hanzhong, a beautiful land known for the Han Pynastyand Three Kingdom's Culture

汉中是国家历史文化名城，两汉三国文化的主要发祥地，名列“中国最美十大城镇”。汉中生物资源丰富，素有“生物资源宝库”之称，也是全国重要的中药材生产基地。

Hanzhong is one of famous historical and cultural cities and the main birthplace of the Han and Three Kingdoms' Culture. It is one of "China's Top 10 Beautiful Cities". Hanzhong is rich in biological resources and enjoys the reputation of "biological resource treasure". It is also an important herb production base in China.

秦巴明珠　生态安康

Ankang, an ecological city like a pearl in Qin-Ba hinterland

安康是我国西部地区重要的清洁能源基地、区域交通枢纽，也是“南水北调”中线工程核心水源区。安康自然资源富集，是全国富硒茶、绞股蓝、魔芋之乡。

Ankang is an important clean energy base and a regional traffic hub in western China. It is also the core water source zone for the middle route of the national "South-to-North Water Diversion Project". Ankang boasts rich natural resources and is the home of selenium-enriched tea, Gynostemma Pentaphyllum and konjac.

雄秦秀楚　最美商洛

Shangluo, a charming city with the Qin's majesty and Chu's beauty

商洛地跨长江、黄河两大流域，为革命老区，有丰富的生物、矿产和旅游资源。现已形成现代材料、现代中药、绿色食品、生态旅游四大特色产业体系。

Straddling the basins of the Yangtze River and the Yellow River, Shangluo is an old revolutionary base and has rich biological, mineral and tourism resources. Today, the city has formed four major specialty industrial systems, namely, modern materials, modern herbs, green food and ecological tourism.

附录二
2013 年以来，
陕西入选“全国十大考古新发现”的考古遗址

Annex II
Shaanxi's Archaeological Sites Listed on China's Annual Top 10 Archaeological Sites Discovered since 2013

2013 年　陕西西安汉长安城北渭桥遗址

Weiqiao Site in Chang'an of the Han, Xi'an, Shaanxi, 2013

渭桥遗址位于西安市北郊汉长安城北渭桥遗址北侧，在此相继发掘出三组七座渭桥。其中一号桥是目前世界上发现的最大的木梁柱桥，也是丝绸之路从汉长安城出发后的第一座桥梁。

Weiqiao Site is located in the north of Chang'an City Site of the Han Dynasty, presently the north suburb of Xi'an City. Altogether seven bridges in three groups were excavated. Bridge No. 1 is the world's biggest wooden beam bridge discovered so far, and the first bridge in the Silk Road after departing Chang'an in the Han Dynasty.

2015 年　陕西宝鸡周原遗址

Zhouyuan Site, Baoji, Shaanxi, 2015

遗址中的建筑遗址是迄今为止规模最大的西周单体建筑基址，为具有殷移民特色的普通“居址—墓葬区”。宝鸡周原遗址的一系列发现，共同构成了对西周都邑型聚落人群构成和社会结构的新认识。

The building in the site has the biggest single foundation of Western Zhou Dynasty discovered so far and features the ordinary "residence-tomb zone" of the migrants of Yin and Shang Dynasties. The discoveries contributed to new cognition of the population and social structure of city communities in the Western Zhou Dynasty.

2016 年　陕西凤翔雍山血池秦汉祭祀遗址

Yongshan Xuechi Sacrifice Site of the Qin and Han Dynasties, Fengxiang, Shaanxi, 2016

该遗址为首次在秦都雍城附近发现的与古文献记载相吻合，时代较早、规模最大、性质明确、持续时间最长，且功能结构趋于完整的国家大型祭祀遗址。

It is the first sacrifice site discovered near Yongcheng, the capital of Qin Kingdom, and complies with ancient records. It features early history, big scale, definite nature, long existence and completeness in function and structure as a large-scale national sacrifice site.

2017 年　陕西高陵杨官寨遗址

Yangguanzhai Site, Gaoling, Shaanxi, 2017

墓葬年代为庙底沟文化时期，是国内首次确认的庙底沟文化大型成人墓地。

The site is a large-sized adult tomb of the Miaodigou Civilization Period confirmed for the first time in China.

2017 年　陕西西安秦汉栎阳城遗址

The Yueyang City Site of Qin and Han Dynasties, Xi'an, Shaanxi, 2017

遗址内首次出土了清晰的“栎阳”陶文，确认了“商鞅变法”发生地正是栎阳。栎阳城是中国城市发展阶段上的重要环节，对研究秦汉都城的规划、中国城市的发展史都有重要价值。

Pottery inscribed with clear characters "Yueyang" were first unearthed at the site, proving "ShangYang's Reform" took place in Yueyang. As an important step in China's city development, Yueyang City is of great value to study the capital planning of the Qin and Han dynasties as well as the evolution history of China's cities.

2018 年　陕西延安芦山峁新石器时代遗址

Lushanmao Neolithic Site, Yan'an, Shaanxi, 2018

该遗址以四座台城式建筑群为核心，面积超过 200 万平方米。四座台城中最大的 “大营盘梁”部分分布着三座院落，由北部一座大型院落和南部两座小型院落构成“品”字形布局。

The site is centered on four Taicheng-style buildings, covering an area of more than 2 million square meters. The largest of the four Taicheng "Da Ying Pan Liang" department is distributed with three courtyards—a large courtyard in the north and two small courtyards in the south, forming a layout of the Chinese character "pin" (品).

2018 年　陕西澄城刘家洼东周遗址

Liujiawa Site of the Eastern Zhou Dynasty, Chengcheng, Shaanxi, 2018

遗址由城址、居址和基地组成，发掘清理出大量青铜器以及金器、玉器、铁器、陶器和漆木器等珍贵文物。推断这里是芮国后期的都城遗址及墓地，该遗址的发现填补了芮国后期历史的空白。

The site, composed of the city part, the residence part and the base of the city, was excavated a large number of valuable cultural relics like bronze, gold, jade, iron, pottery and lacquered wood artifacts. It is inferred that this is the capital city site and cemetery in later period of Ruiguo (one of vassal states during the Western Zhou Dynasty and the Spring and Autumn Period), which fills the gap in the history of this period. The discovery of the site has filled a gap in the history of late Rui.

2019 年　陕西神木石峁遗址皇城台

The Imperial Platform of Shimao Site, Shenmu, Shaanxi, 2019

石峁遗址皇城台是内城和外城重重拱卫的核心，或已具备早期“宫城”性质，是目前东亚地区保存最好、规模最大的早期宫城建筑，展现了黄土高原上一处神秘王国都邑的极致辉煌。

Surrounded and protected by the inner and outer cities, the Imperial Platform of Shimao Site may have already functioned as an early imperial city. It is the best preserved and the largest early palace complex in East Asia, showing the ultimate glory of the mysterious kingdom capital on the Loess Plateau.

2020 年　陕西西安少陵原十六国大墓

Sixteen Kingdoms Tombs in Shaolingyuan Plateau, Xi'an，Shaanxi, 2020

遗址有三座规格巨大、形制特殊、结构完整的十六国时期高等级墓葬，出土土雕建筑、壁画以及彩绘陶俑等，是国内迄今为止发现的规模最大的十六国时期高等级墓葬。

Three high-level tombs of the Sixteen Kingdoms Period were excavated with huge size, peculiar shape and complete structure, along with earth sculpture architecture, murals and painted pottery figurines. They are the largest high-level tombs of the Sixteen Kingdoms Period discovered in China up to now.

2021 年　陕西西安江村大墓

Jiangcun Village Tomb, Xi'an, Shaanxi, 2021

遗址的发掘确定了霸陵的准确位置，解决了西汉十一陵的名位问题。为西汉帝陵制度形成、发展、演变的研究提供了翔实的考古资料，为中国古代帝王陵墓制度的深入研究奠定了基础。

The excavation of Jiangcun Village Tomb helped to determine the exact location of the Ba Mausoleum and solved the problem of the name and position of 11 mausoleums of the Western Han Dynasty. In addition, the excavation has provided detailed archaeological data for the study of the formation, development and evolution of the imperial mausoleum system in the Western Han Dynasty, and laid foundation for the in-depth study of the imperial mausoleum system in ancient China.

附录三
巧夺天工的陕西国宝级文物

Annex Ⅲ
Shaanxi Cultural Relics with Exquisite Workmanship

秦始皇帝陵博物院 铜车马

Emperor QinShiHuang's Mauso Leum Site,
Copper Carriages of Emperor

陕西历史博物馆 兽首玛瑙杯

Shaanxi History Museum,
Beast Head-shaped
Agate Cup

宝鸡青铜器博物院 西周墙盘

Baoji Bronze Ware Museum,
Western Zhou's Qiang Basin

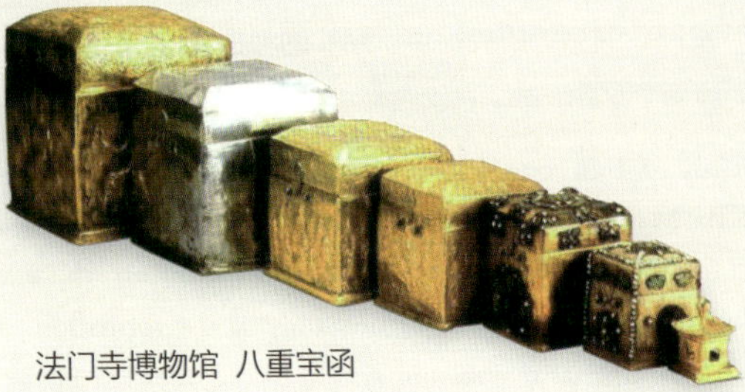

法门寺博物馆 八重宝函

Famen Temple Museum ,
Eight Cases

法门寺博物馆 铜浮屠

Famen Temple Museum,
Copper pagoda

西安碑林博物馆　景云铜钟

Xi'an Beilin Museum,
Jingyun Bronze Bell

西安碑林博物馆　大秦景教流行中国碑

Xi'an Beilin Museum,
Stele on Nestorianism from Eastern Roman Empire's Spread in China

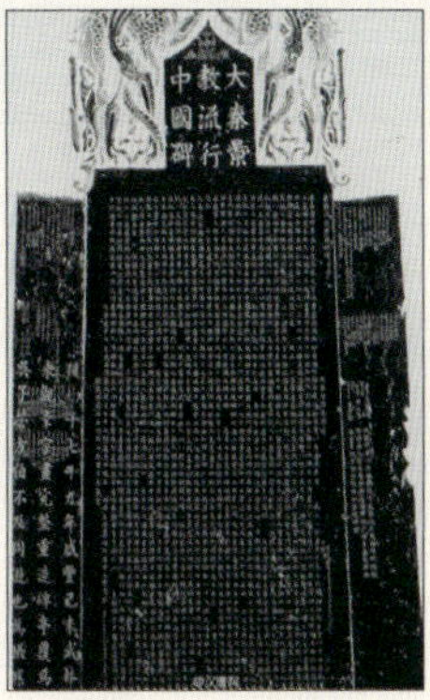

宝鸡青铜器博物院　何尊

Baoji Bronze Museum,
HeZun

陕西历史博物馆　淳化大鼎

Shaanxi History Museum ,
Chunhua Caldron

法门寺博物馆　银花双轮十二环锡杖

Famen Temple Museum,
A Monk's Cane with Silver Flowers and 12 Rings

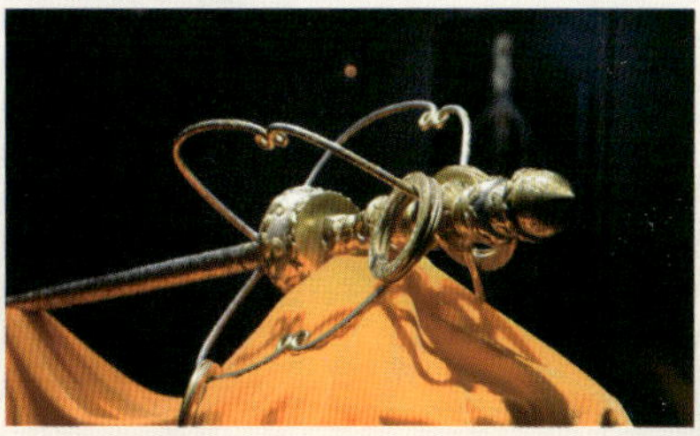

陕西茂陵博物馆　茂陵石雕

Shaanxi Maoling Mausoleum Museum,
Stone Sculpture of Mausoleum Museum

陕西历史博物馆　舞马衔杯仿皮囊式银壶

Shaanxi History Museum,
Leather Bag-shaped Silver Pot with a Dancing Horse Holding a Cup in Its Mouth

附录四
陕西第一批“国家级非物质文化遗产”名录

Annex Ⅳ
The First Batch of "National Intangible Cultural Heritage" in Shaanxi

Egong Shadow Play 阿宫腔

Heyang String Puppet Show 合阳提线木偶戏

Southern Shaanxi Local Opera 汉调二黄

Xi'an Drum Music 西安鼓乐

Shangluo Flower Drum 商洛花鼓

Shadow Play 弦板腔

Fengxiang Clay Sculpture 凤翔泥塑

Lantian Puhua Folk Music 蓝田普化水会音乐

Shaanxi Opera 秦腔

Huayin Laoqiang Opera 华阴老腔

Yaozhou Kiln Ceramics Firing and Manufacturing Skills 耀州窑陶瓷烧制技艺

Ansai Wrist Drum 安塞腰鼓

Northern Shaanxi Yangge Performance
陕北秧歌

Fengxiang Xylograph New Year Pictures
凤翔木版年画

Ziyang Folk Song
紫阳民歌

Sacrificial Rites at the Mausoleum of the Yellow Emperor
黄帝陵祭典

Chengcheng Yaotou Ceramics Firing and Manufacturing Skills
澄城尧头陶瓷烧制技艺

Luochuan Bouncing Drum Dance (Biegu)
洛川蹩鼓

Ansai Paper cutting
安塞剪纸

Yulin Folk Tune
榆林小曲

Huaxian County shadow Puppet
华县皮影戏

Hanzhong Local Opera
汉调桄桄

Northern Shaanxi Storytelling
陕北说书

Baoji Building Sacred Fire
宝鸡社火

附录五 陕西特产

Annex Ⅴ Shaanxi Specialties

临潼石榴

Lintong Pomegranate

石榴相传为西汉张骞出使西域时引进的，距今已有 2000 多年的历史。临潼石榴皮红个儿大，皮薄籽满，色泽鲜艳，味美可口。

Lintong Pomegranate, having a history of more than 2,000 years, features a thin and red peel, large size, bright color and delicious taste. It is said that pomegranate was introduced to China when Zhang Qian visited the western countries along the Silk Road in the Han Dynasty.

西凤酒

Xifeng Liquor

西凤酒

XI FENG LIQUOR

西凤酒产于宝鸡市凤翔区，因凤翔位于关中西部，故称西凤酒。西凤酒距今已有 2600 多年的历史，是我国八大名酒之一，远销海内外。

Xifeng Liquor is produced in Fengxiang, a county to the west of Guanzhong. With a history of more than 2,600 years, the liquor is one of China's eight famous liquors and widely sold across the world.

陕北红枣

Northern Shaanxi Red Date

陕北红枣主要产于黄河沿岸的宜川、延川、清涧、吴堡、佳县、神木、府谷等地，它以果大、核小、皮薄、肉厚、味醇、油性大、色红、酸甜可口，含丰富的蛋白质、维生素、矿物质闻名于世。

Northern Shaanxi Red Dates, mainly produced in Yichuan, Yanchuan, Qingjian, Wubu, Jiaxian, Shenmu, Fugu and other counties along the Yellow River, are world-famous due to the big size, small core, thin peel, thick pulp, pure flavor, high oil content, red color, nice taste, and rich content of protein, vitamin and mineral.

稠酒

Choujiu Wine

稠酒又名“黄桂稠酒”，是一种古老名酒，盛唐时期朝野上下无不饮之。党和国家领导人多次用它来招待和宴请贵宾。郭沫若曾赞誉它“不像酒，胜似酒”。

Choujiu Wine, a famous ancient wine also known as "Huanggui Choujiu Wine", was quite popular in the Tang Dynasty. Leaders entertained domestic and foreign guests with the wine. "It doesn't taste like wine, but its taste is better than wine" was Guo Moruo's praise for the wine.

陕南茶叶

Southern Shaanxi Tea

陕茶主要种植区域在巴山北麓陕南三市所辖的 28 个县（区）。著名品牌有汉中仙毫、紫阳富硒茶、商南泉茗、定军茗眉、汉水银梭、午子仙毫，以及陕南茶叶制作的著名黑茶系列——泾渭茯茶等。

The north slope of the Bashan Mountain, 28 counties and districts under the jurisdiction of three Southern Shaanxi cities are the main tea planting areas of Shaanxi. The famous tea brands include Hanzhong Xianhao, Ziyang Se-enriched Tea, Shangnan Quanming, Dingjun Mingmei, Hanshui Yinsuo and Wuzi Xianhao, and the renowned black tea Jingwei Fu Tea made of southern Shaanxi tea leaves.

核桃

Walnut

陕西渭北一带和商洛地区是著名的核桃之乡，年产量为全国第一。核桃富含蛋白质、维生素、矿物质，对人体有较高的保健作用。

The northern region of the Weihe River and the Shangluo prefecture are the famous producing areas of walnuts and rank China's No. 1 in annual yield. Walnuts are healthy because of its high content of protein, vitamins and minerals.

苹果
Apple

陕西苹果是全球知名品牌，已经被定为国礼，产量、品质均为中国第一。因为陕西的渭北平原和黄土高原地带日照充足，昼夜温差适当，最适宜苹果生长，故陕西苹果酥脆香甜，微酸爽口，汁多味正。

Shaanxi Apples, a world-famous brand, are honored as a national gift thanks to their supreme production and quality in China. The Weibei Plain and Loess Plateau of Shaanxi are the most appropriate region for growing apple trees thanks to the sufficient sunshine and moderate diurnal amplitude. Thus, the apples are sweet, crisp, dainty, juicy and flavorful.

中华猕猴桃
Actinidia Chinensis

中华猕猴桃小的似核桃，大的如鹅卵，皮色褐绿，内瓤翠绿，清香酸甜，营养价值较高。它除了可以食鲜果，还可加工成果汁、果酒和果酱等。

Actinidia Chinensis (Chinese kiwi fruit), is the size of walnuts or goose eggs. With breen peel and green pulp, the fragrant and sweet fruit has high nutrition value. It can also be processed into juice, wine and jam.

临潼火晶柿子
Lintong Fire Crystal Persimmon

火晶柿子是临潼特有的柿树品种。柿子个儿小色红，晶莹光亮，皮薄无核，深受国内外游客欢迎。

Lintong Fire Crystal Persimmon, a unique persimmon in Lintong featuring small size, red color, bright appearance, thin peel and small core, is greatly favored by domestic and foreign guests.

富平柿饼

Fuping Dried Persimmon

富平柿饼又称富平合儿饼。以富平县自产的优质柿子制成。形似圆月，肉红透明，无子，凝霜后，白里透红、皮脆柔软、清甜爽口，因两个相对成一合而得名。富平柿饼营养丰富，具有润肺、补血、健胃、止咳等药理功能。

It is also called Fuping Dual Pie and made of high quality persimmon produced in Fuping. It is a round, transparent flesh-colored candied fruit without seeds. The frosty ones are reddish white, crisp in peel and soft in pulp. Two persimmons are placed oppositely in a package, thus called Dual Pie. It is nutritious and has a medicinal effect on lungs, blood and stomach and relieves coughs.

秦椒

Qin Pepper

秦椒素有“椒中之王”的美称，是陕西一项大宗出口商品，畅销国际市场。

Qin Pepper, known as "the king of peppers", is a sort of bulk export of Shaanxi and widely sold in global market.

陕北小米

Northern Shaanxi Millet

陕北小米是指产于陕北延安、榆林一带的小米。陕北地区光热资源充足，昼夜温差大，因而盛产谷子。谷子成熟后稍经加工，即成黄灿灿、香喷喷的小米。得益于得天独厚的自然条件，陕北小米养分积累多，营养价值高，是极具特色的陕西特产。

It refers to the millet produced in Yan'an and Yulin of northern Shaanxi. The sufficient light, heat and temperature difference between day and night contribute to the growth of millet plants. The matured plants become the yellow and sweet millet through simple processing. Thanks to the advantageous natural conditions, the millet absorbs plentiful nutrient and boasts rich nutrition. It is a highly recognizable Shaanxi specialty.

附录六 陕西精华旅游线路

Annex Ⅵ Best Tourist Routes in Shaanxi

1 日游 One-day Tour

线路一 西安古都一日游（市内） Route A: One-day Tour in Ancient Capital Xi'an (Downtown)

Bell and Drum Towers—Shaanxi History Museum—Xi'an Stele Forest—Xi'an City Wall—Shuyuanmen Cultural Street

线路二 西安古都一日游（市内） Route B: One-day Tour in Ancient Capital Xi'an (Downtown)

Giant Wild Goose Pagoda—Tang Paradise—Small Wild Goose Pagoda—Great Mosque—Courtyard of Family Gao—Fangshang Muslim Snack Street

线路三 东线一日游 Route C: One-day Eastward Tour

Emperor QinShiHuang's Mausoleum site—Huaqing Pond—Mausoleum of Emperor Qinshihuang—Banpo Museum

线路四 西岳华山一日游 Route D: One-day Tour to Huashan Mountains

线路五 西线一日游 Route E: One-day Westward Tour

Famen Temple—Qianling Mausoleum—Princess Yongtai's Tomb

2日游 Two-day Tour

线路一 东线二日游 Route A: Two-day Eastward Tour

第一日 D1

西安—华山  —韩城 

Xi'an—Huashan Mountain—Hancheng

第二日 D2

党家村  司马迁祠  韩城文庙  黄河龙门  —西安

Dangjia Village—Sima Qian Temple—Confucius Temple in Hancheng—Longmen of the Yellow River—Xi'an

线路二 西线二日游 Route B: Two-day Westward Tour

第一日 D1

西安—乾陵  法门寺  —宝鸡

Xi'an—Qianling Mausoleum— Famen Temple—Baoji

第二日 D2

宝鸡青铜器博物院  楼观台  —西安

Baoji Bronze Ware Museum—Louguan Platform—Xi'an

附录七
陕西小吃

Annex Ⅶ
Shaanxi Snacks

→
灌汤包子
Steamed Stuffed Bun with Secret Soup

↓
粉蒸肉
Steamed Pork with Rice Flour

←
麻酱凉皮
Sesame Rice Slices

↙
羊肉泡馍
Pita Bread Soaked in Lamb Soup

←
肉丸胡辣汤
Meatballs Spicy Soup

↑
乾县豆腐脑
Jellied Bean Curd of Qianxian County

↓
大米凉皮
Cold Rice Slices

↑
金线油塔
Crispy Fried Noodles

↗
酸汤水饺
Dumplings in Sour Soup

↑
腊汁肉夹馍
Meat Sandwiched in Pie

←
𰻞𰻞面
Shaanxi Handmade Noodles

→
甑糕
Glutinous Rice and Date Cake

↓
荞面饸饹
Buckwheat Vermicelli

↘
搟面皮
Processed Noodles

↑
水盆羊肉
Mutton in Water Basin

→
锅盔辣子
Flour Pancake with Hot Pepper

↗
臊子面
Minced Pork Noodles

←
柿子饼
Dried Persimmon

→
豆花泡馍
Steamed Bun with Bean Curd

→
黄米糕
Yellow Rice Cake

↗
洋芋擦擦
Steamed Potato Slices

→
黄馍馍
Yellow Steamed Bun

↑
菜豆腐
Vegetarian Toufu

↑
炕炕馍
Sesame Seed Cake

↗
热米皮
Hot Rice Slices

图书在版编目（CIP）数据

2022中国陕西 / 陕西省人民政府新闻办公室编 . —西安 : 陕西人民出版社 , 2022.4

ISBN 978-7-224-14521-2

Ⅰ . ① 2… Ⅱ . ①陕… Ⅲ . ①陕西—概况 Ⅳ . ① K924.1

中国版本图书馆 CIP 数据核字（2022）第 063009 号

责任编辑 | 关　宁
韩　琳
翻　　译 | 杨冬敏
杨　敏

2022 中国陕西

编　　者	陕西省人民政府新闻办公室
出版发行	陕西新华出版传媒集团　陕西人民出版社 （西安北大街 147 号　邮编：710003）
印　　刷	陕西金和印务有限公司
开　　本	787mm × 1092mm　1/16
印　　张	10.5
字　　数	150 千字
版　　次	2022 年 4 月第 1 版
印　　次	2022 年 4 月第 1 次印刷
书　　号	ISBN 978-7-224-14521-2
定　　价	68.00 元